Matchbox

Official
50th Anniversary
Commemorative
Edition

Matc

Official 50th Anniversary

Text by Richard J. Scholl

hb⊙x

Commemorative Edition

UNIVERSE

First published in the United States of America in 2002
By UNIVERSE PUBLISHING

A Division of Rizzoli International Publications, Inc.
300 Park Avenue South
New York, NY 10010

Library of Congress Control Number: 2001096434

An extension of this copyright page can be found on pages 264–267.

Universe Editor: Terence Maikels
Copy Editors: Laura Magzis, Corey Sabourin

Photographs of cars by James Portellos and Nigel McMillan
Designed by David Larkin

Printed in England

Contents

Introduction

I can tell you exactly when I became a Matchbox collector. It was June 28, 1997. I was at the Matchbox Convention in Hershey, Pennsylvania. That's where I found my prize—a double-decker, horse-drawn trolley with a Lipton Tea advertisement on the side. I paid $35 for it.

I had always called this the "Lipton Tea Wagon," whatever its correct name was. I had never owned it, but I had never forgotten it since I first saw it in the display case at Mitchell's in Wilmington, Delaware, where for several years I went on my Friday night pilgrimage to see the new Matchbox cars while my parents did the grocery shopping. I didn't know why, but the Lipton Tea Wagon called to me. In part, it spoke to my fascination with history and vehicles, and like most kids I was fascinated by the size and the detail. However, it was part of the Models of Yesteryear and had a price of more than two dollars, far beyond the reach of my grade-school allowance. My mother, knowing how much I liked it (how could she not? I'd climb back in the station wagon talking about nothing else), promised to buy it for me for Christmas. But when she went back to Mitchell's, they had sold every one, as had every other store she called. So, the Lipton Tea Wagon slipped through our fingers then, and I think my mother was more disappointed than I was.

Now, some people who know me would be surprised to think that I have called myself a "collector" for only five years. My Matchbox cars were my favorite toys growing up. Still, when asked what my favorite toy is—which happens almost daily—I always say Matchbox without hesitation. Matchbox featured prominently in my letters to the North Pole, and I lovingly parked my collection every night in shoe-box garages. Hours would pass after homework and on weekends in creating elaborate worlds with my admittedly eclectic fleet.

Sometimes my cars opened a window to the past, as my prized Models of Yesteryear brought my grandparents' young days alive. My grandfather, grandmother, and great aunts recognized many of my favorites—and had actually ridden in some of the originals, a fact that was always awe-inspiring.

Sometimes the living room floor was transformed into a giant farm. (Tractors held a particular fascination for a while.) On any given day there were races, auto shows, and the acting

out of a broad range of stories, all centering around one or more of my always-changing favorites. And, of course, there were the inevitable spectacular pileups involving every car I owned and requiring the noisy arrival—sound effects provided by me—of all the rescue vehicles.

Throughout my life, no matter where I've lived, I've never been without my Matchbox cars. I first started hauling them along with me wherever I went to keep them out of the reach of my two younger brothers. Oh, they had their own precious collections, but they certainly weren't above "borrowing" a particular favorite of mine—never to be seen again. What began as an act of strategic defense, though, became a comfort and an inspiration. I liked having my Matchbox cars around. So, they were with me throughout college, in my first tiny apartment in Brooklyn, and they're still with me today. I still take them out and play with them, though, I suppose, in a more adult way. By serious standards, my collection is certainly modest, yet each Matchbox vehicle—trains, trailers, cars of all varieties—is still vividly associated with specific and very happy memories.

I know I'm not alone. Matchbox cars have for the past fifty years been one of the truest embodiments of our culture's collective fascination with vehicles. We are in love with going and moving and doing—and cars represent that romance and sense of freedom. They also reflect the apex of human creativity and ingenuity with their combination of style and raw power. As manufactured items, completely man-made, cars speak to the distinctly human gift of creating something tangible, valuable, beautiful, and practical from something as ephemeral as an idea. That defining human characteristic, along with the ability to share a piece history, revisit our childhoods and share the fun with others, is central to adults' love for Matchbox cars.

As toys for kids, Matchbox cars have always been very nearly perfect. They are inexpensive, remarkably realistic and detailed, but most importantly, they provide a springboard for creative play. The imagination doesn't merely give life to toys; when developed and nurtured, it is an invaluable gift, allowing children to create possibility throughout life—to become truly themselves. Matchbox cars have been part of that process for millions of kids.

As for me, I still didn't become a Matchbox collector when I bought my Lipton Tea Wagon. As soon as I bought it, I walked into the lobby of the hotel and called my parents. I told them what I'd purchased and we laughed about my trips to Mitchell's and my undiminished affection for Matchbox cars, even at my age. My mother insisted on sending a check immediately, saying she was not going to be stopped from fulfilling a promise made so many years ago, and she made me promise to bring "our" Lipton Tea Wagon with me the next time I visited. It was in that moment that I finally experienced what every true Matchbox collector knows: it's not the car, it's the connection.

This book is a celebration of all of our connections with and through Matchbox over half a century. At fifty, Matchbox is still one of the most vital and compelling toy brands in the world. It is a true classic, an indelible part of our culture—and no matter how old you are, still an awful lot of fun.

CHRISTOPHER BYRNE, A.K.A. THE TOY GUY™

NEW YORK CITY, MAY 2002

Foreword

As Matchbox® celebrates its 50th anniversary, it's appropriate first and foremost to recognize what a remarkable feat this is. Very few brands stand the test of time. Most become victims of the latest trend or intense competition, the inability to adapt to changing times or, frankly, poor management. But the brand Matchbox stands tall in the very small company of American brands that have weathered recessions, depressions, wars and the continued advances in technology. For Matchbox, this means that a company known principally for its die-cast models has survived video, electronic and computer games and many other toys and products directed at the kids who have been loyal to Matchbox for generations.

In reaching its 50th birthday, Matchbox joins a number of other venerable American brands, some of which are over 100 years old. And, interestingly, many of them have been associated with Matchbox in some way over the years, usually by authorizing models bearing their official graphics. These include Anheuser-Busch, Disney, Harley-Davidson, Jack Daniel's, McDonald's, Coca-Cola, Pepsi-Cola, Mack Trucks, Peterbilt, Freightliner, Caterpillar, Texaco, Shell, Sunoco, and the big three automakers—DaimlerChrysler, Ford, and General Motors. Pretty good company, indeed.

Born amidst the euphoria and reconstruction of the post World War II era, "Matchbox" was invented at Lesney Products and has since been owned by three other companies through the years: Universal, Tyco, and now Mattel. Mattel is commemorating the 50th anniversary of Matchbox in a variety of ways, including sponsorship of this fifty-year history book.

Mattel is also issuing a series of fifty models called "Matchbox® Across America 50th Birthday Series." The series consists of a collection of fifty vehicles, each representing one of the fifty United States, celebrating fifty years of Matchbox history. Each model will bear graphics of a U.S. state, as well as a miniature replica of the state's license plate.

Mattel will celebrate the Matchbox 50th birthday in many other ways, as well. For example, traveling displays of Matchbox models are making their way throughout the United States. This road show ends in New York with a big birthday party. The annual Matchbox collector show that traditionally takes place in Hershey, Pennsylvania, will also be in New York City, in conjunction with the party.

Collectors who know something about Matchbox history may be wondering why the year 1952 was determined to be the origin of the Matchbox brand. Although Lesney Products was founded in 1947, it was in 1952 that Jack Odell of Lesney created the first Matchbox model for his daughter to take to school. Of course, no one could have anticipated what an amazing phenomenon Matchbox would become.

Most of us grew up with Matchbox toys, which were popular not only in the United Kingdom (the birthplace of Matchbox) and the United States, but all through the world, including Germany, France, and Australia.

Along with baseball cards and marbles, Matchbox die-cast vehicles represented millions of kids' first experience with collecting. And, like the baseball cards we kept in our shoe boxes, Matchbox vehicles often became more valuable as they got older. They were suddenly transformed from toys into the realm of collectibles, often commanding stratospheric prices. As a result, many of today's collectors tend to think of all Matchbox models as collectible.

This book provides some insight into why Matchbox models often became coveted collector items, such as certain variations in color when the factory ran out of a certain color of paint. But, unlike most of the books that cover Matchbox history, the focus here is not on cataloging the many models in famed series like the Matchbox® 1-75 models or Models of Yesteryear® series. Instead, this book attempts to take you behind the scenes as we trace the major figures, decisions, triumphs, and pitfalls that make the history of Matchbox so fascinating.

Whether you are an avid Matchbox collector or a beginner—or somewhere in between like me—I hope you enjoy the fifty-year odyssey of

Matchbox. The toys that became collector items evolved from playthings that British retailers initially scorned to one of the most significant brands, toy businesses, and collector traditions of the twentieth century. Along the way, Matchbox literally became an important part of many children's and adults' lives. From the rather crude toys of yesteryear to the highly intricate models recently produced by Matchbox Collectibles®, there has always been something special—even magical—about Matchbox.

I can only hope that some of that magic comes through in the pages of this book.

RICHARD J. SCHOLL

1962 Volkswagen, Fiftieth Anniversary, 2002

The Origin of a New Species: The Die-Cast Brand Every Kid Collected

The Matchbox legacy was born of coincidence and adversity combined with determination, ingenuity, and the love of a father for his daughter.

Let's begin with coincidence.

The co-founders of Lesney—the company that invented the Matchbox® brand—were Leslie Smith and Rodney Smith. They had the same last name, but they weren't related. However, they were born about six months apart in 1917 and 1918, and they became boyhood friends. After attending the Central School in Enfield, they lost touch with each other, but their paths crossed again in 1940. They talked about possibly going into some kind of engineering business together after the war. After both served admirably in the English Royal Navy during World War II, they were "demobbed," which is roughly the American equivalent of being honorably discharged.

Leslie Smith and Rodney Smith entered into a partnership called Lesney Products. The name "Lesney" combines the first three letters of Leslie's name and the last three of Rodney's. The word "Products" was chosen simply because the two entrepreneurs had no earthly idea what they would actually produce. It was a good thing, therefore, that they "kept their day jobs," as the saying goes.

Leslie burned the candle at both ends, working for the J. Raymond Wilson Company by day—where he purchased carpets and textiles and handled overseas orders. This was the same company that employed Leslie before the war. By night, he maintained the financial records of Lesney Products for several years until the fledgling enterprise sprouted wings and could afford him full-time.

Rodney Smith put food on the table by working at the engineering firm of Die Cast and Machine Tools in North London, whose principal business was manufacturing die-casting equipment. This was a very wise career choice for the young co-founder of Lesney Products for two reasons. First, he learned about the process of casting products made from dies. Even more important, Rodney met John W. "Jack" Odell, who not only would soon contribute his design and casting skills to Lesney Products, but also would actually design the first Matchbox models.

Moreover, Die Cast and Machine Tools was one of the companies that began making die-cast toys—including cars—after the war. There weren't many toys on store shelves at this time. The war had required many companies—including toy manufacturers—to produce products to support the war effort. At any rate, both Rodney Smith and Jack Odell were working for the company at a time when it was producing cowboy guns under the "Lone Star" brand, trains, and other toys, many of which were marketed by the Crescent Toy Company.

A Dream Born of a Shoestring Budget and a Determined Trio

Leslie Smith and Rodney Smith pooled their resources—consisting of the gratuities they received for their service during the war—and funded their new enterprise with roughly 600 pounds. They used part of the money to buy a condemned building, an old tavern called "Rifleman" in Edmonton, London. They also purchased used die-casting machinery from Rodney's former employer, Die Cast and Machine Tools. The company focused on manufacturing small die-cast products to help support the reconstruction of London after the destruction wrought by the war. Lesney's first order was for 20,000 string cutters, "which were crude components made up of an old razor blade and a die-cast holder."[1] This project gave the company the traction it needed to begin to grow.

The Smiths were soon joined by Jack Odell, an engineer who had served in the Royal Army Service Corp and the Royal Electrical Mechanical Engineers during World War II; he was involved in making tanks. After the war, Odell purchased some Army surplus machinery on the strength of orders he had already received. He wanted to set up his casting business in his mother's garage, but this wasn't permitted by the local council. Odell had heard about the Smiths' building and went to see them.

The Smiths allowed Odell to set up shop in their building because he agreed to pay their £2 weekly rent. Based on the first tool he created, Odell received his first casting order from the General Electric Company of the United Kingdom for 10,000 hook ceiling plates. The Smiths were so impressed by Odell's success, they asked him to become a full partner in their enterprise. Odell agreed to join them.

The responsibilities of each man were clearly defined: Leslie Smith—who continued working part-time at the J. Raymond Wilson Company— was in charge of sales and bookkeeping. Rodney Smith was responsible for die casting and Jack Odell used his exceptional design skills to make the molds. Odell began experimenting with an innovative tooling method for pressure die-casting that would soon give Lesney a major manufacturing advantage. He developed a process that all but eliminated the need to remove excess metal from castings.

By 1948, the burgeoning firm of Lesney Products had thirty-five different industrial moulds and dies and eight employees, in addition to the three directors. However, no sooner did Lesney begin to achieve modest success than the company faced its first round of adversity.

In England at this time, businesses customarily decreased their inventories toward the end of each calendar year to minimize the tax they would pay on the inventory they held on January 1. This meant that many companies— including Lesney—suffered from slack demand in the last couple months of the year. But, once again, good fortune smiled on Lesney Products.

They received an order from M.Y. Dart to make a die-cast piece of a toy cap gun. This was a turning point because the Smiths and Odell realized that they could make toys during slow periods. Jack Odell said, "We got one or two Dinky toys and we made similar ones for about a third of the price . . . and they sold extremely well." The first three models were a Diesel Road Roller, Cement Mixer, and Crawler Tractor. These first three Lesney toys were not only far cheaper than the Dinky models, but they were of comparable quality. (See Chapter 10 for the story of Dinky, a giant in die-cast history.) "The toys were packed one dozen to a box and Leslie Smith secured a contract, initially with Woolworths, but later with national wholesalers."[1]

Early Bread Bait Press, 1954

Of course, Lesney's solution to its end-of-year slowdown in business was nothing novel. Die Cast and Machine Tools—former employer of both Rodney Smith and Jack Odell—was among the companies that turned to making toys and other die-cast products when business was slow. Lesney imitated these companies and, in 1948, the first toys by Lesney made their way into small local shops in London. Lesney was incorporated on March 9, 1949.

Although merchandisers from the large retailers weren't initially interested in Lesney and its new toys, both the small shop owners and local children loved the Lesney creations. Unfortunately, Lesney's momentum was stopped in its tracks by the Korean War. From 1950 to 1952, the British government said that zinc could only be used for essentials. Prior to the ban, Lesney issued its largest toy to date: the Prime Mover, which pulled an open trailer with a bulldozer on the trailer, as well as ramps for loading and unloading the bulldozer. While the zinc ban was in place, Lesney made only "Jumbo the Elephant," a wind-up toy crafted of tin.

In 1950, anticipating the upcoming Festival of Britain, Lesney had invested some of its profits into new molds to make the Royal State Coach. But the subsequent ban on using zinc to make toys prevented the company from going into production.

The Departure of Rodney Smith and the Creation of the First "Matchbox" Model

Rodney Smith was so discouraged by the war-inflicted ban that he left the firm and turned to chicken and duck breeding. After a series of business failures—including pig breeding and "dredging up weeds from the River Thames and selling them to Woolworths as floral decoration,"[1] Rodney worked briefly for another die-cast company and then moved to Australia. In the meantime, Lesney had "built up a good stockpile of zinc before the embargo" and landed an automotive contract that helped revive their sagging enterprise. The war ended, the embargo was lifted and Lesney decided to produce the royal coach it had made dies for in late 1950.

Large Prime Mover with Trailer and Bulldozer, 1950. (In 1956, the bulldozer became a miniature.)

The famous Lesney coach is one of the most interesting stories in Matchbox history. King George VI died in February of 1952 and the die-cast tooling Lesney had developed included a king and queen inside the coach. Queen Elizabeth II would be riding to her coronation alone in early June of 1953. Lesney literally cut the king off at his knees so only the queen appeared to be riding in the coach. The large model of the coach was "a great success with over 33,000 pieces sold." The following year, a miniature version of the coach "was a phenomenal success with over one million pieces being sold."[1] The success of the Lesney Coronation Coach was a milestone in the history of miniature die-casting.

The year 1952 is noteworthy for another event so significant; it was considered the birth of "Matchbox." Now flush with cash, Lesney turned its sights on "creating a range of miniature die-cast models." Jack Odell's breakthrough was a "completed brass prototype of a small road roller." Odell said, "My oldest daughter had just started school and the kids were restricted in what they . . . could play with. The school only allowed them to take a matchbox-sized container to school." She tried "putting the Coronation Coach inside her box," but "it would not go; and that rang a bell with me." Odell realized that if he "could make a model or toy that would go inside her box, she could take that to school." Odell "gave her the brass roller for her box and all the kids came round that night and they wanted one too." This opened Jack Odell's eyes to the idea "that there was an immediate market for miniature toys."[1]

The idea of having miniatures packaged and sold in a box sized for matches wasn't a novel concept since small German wooden dolls and furniture had been packaged in matchboxes as

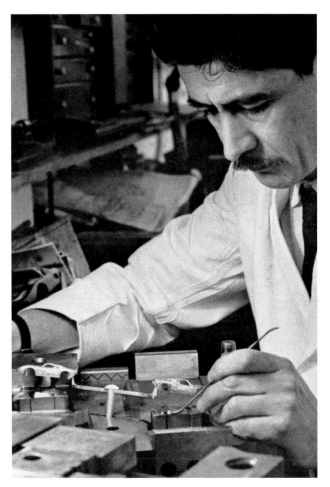

Jack Odell at work in the tool room preparing molds for the Matchbox series.

The Alliance Between the Kohnstams and Lesney Products Ushers in an Era of Explosive Growth

By Christmas of 1953, Lesney management realized that they were squarely in the toy business. However, to grow, they would need many business dimensions they didn't have, including a marketing and sales force and storage facilities. Unable or unwilling to invest in these operations, instead they farmed them out. Specifically, they turned to a firm called Moko because of its considerable experience in marketing toys.

Moko was a company founded by Moses Kohnstam. And the company name was formed in a manner similar to Lesney: the first two letters of his first name (MO) and the first two letters of his last name (KO). Although he is believed to have been born and raised in Czechoslovakia, Kohnstam came to England from Nuremburg, Germany, where he had a thriving business as a toy wholesaler in the small town of Furth, near Nuremburg. His company was a natural fit for Lesney because Moko primarily served the needs of small toy manufacturers, including packaging, warehousing, advertising, distribution, and even financing.

In exchange for these invaluable services, Kohnstam often negotiated for a percentage of the selling price, so Moko had equity in the companies they worked with. But Kohnstam also gained another valuable trade-off: the toys he distributed often carried the Moko name, so his company had visibility among the retailers. After Moses Kohnstam's death in 1912, the business was carried on by his three sons: Emil, Julius, and Willi. In the thirties, Julius and Emil used profits from selling dolls and German toys to help Jews escape Nazi tyranny in Germany. Julius Kohnstam's son, Richard, served in World War II. And Richard was running the Kohnstam business in 1953 when the historic deal was struck with Lesney Products.

early as the 1920s. But it was a new wrinkle in the world of die-casting. Jack Odell "picked up a box of matches made by the Norvic Match Co. Ltd." of Susice, Czechoslovakia. He opened the box and put the prototype he had created for his daughter inside. Leslie Smith said, "We liked this Scandinavian type design and that was the birth of 'Matchbox.' "[1]

By 1953, when the Korean War ended, the Lesney line consisted of eighteen toys. But the product line had no central theme. In addition to die-cast replicas of vehicles like the Caterpillar bulldozer (1948) and the prime mover with trailer and bulldozer (1950), the product line was a motley assortment that included mechanical animals and even a fishing novelty item. Fortunately, the company found its direction through bottom-line performance: its wheeled vehicles were simply more successful than other products.

Moko would provide financial backing and package and distribute the Lesney toys, ultimately becoming the only distributor of Lesney toys worldwide. The Kohnstams were very shrewd businessmen and they, not Lesney, registered the trademark "Matchbox," without bothering to inform Leslie Smith and Jack Odell. After the Lesney directors expressed their indignation over the Kohnstams' presumptuous act, the Matchbox name was re-registered under both companies and ownership of the name was split fifty-fifty between Moko and Lesney.

The Aveling Barford Road Roller

In 1954, the Kohnstam stand at the Harrogate Toy Fair proudly displayed the first four Matchbox miniatures—The Aveling Barford Road Roller, the Muir Hill Site Dumper, the Cement Mixer, and the Massey-Harris Tractor. The toy wholesalers said they couldn't sell the miniatures. But when kids saw "that they could at last buy a toy for 1s. 6d. (7.5p)," the equivalent of a few cents, they began buying the Matchbox toys and, suddenly, the wholesalers wanted "hundreds of gross."[1] Since there are 144 items in one gross, this represented a significant boost in business for Lesney.

The Glorious End of the Exciting Beginning

The Matchbox legacy was born of coincidence: the chance meetings of Leslie and Rodney Smith before and after World War II and the fact that Jack Odell's daughter and her schoolmates weren't permitted to bring anything to school unless it fit into a matchbox.

The Matchbox phenomenon was fueled by adversity: the seasonal end-of-the-year decline in die-casting business due to anticipation of taxes on inventory in the New Year.

The illustrious fifty-year history of the Matchbox name also took root in the fertile soil of determination. Leslie Smith, Rodney Smith, and Jack Odell wanted to make something of their lives—to push their dream as far as it could go, even if Rodney left the business prematurely and wasn't around when Matchbox ultimately became a household name.

And isn't it apropos that the origin of a legacy that has brought joy to millions of children was ignited by the love of a father for his daughter? Jack Odell wanted his daughter—who had just started school—to bring something special in her matchbox. That miniature road roller was a big hit with the kids in her class. After Jack Odell cast a few more models for the kids, the now legendary Matchbox 1-75 series was born. Soon the popularity of Matchbox would spread throughout England, into America, and all over the world. Every kid would grow up collecting Matchbox toys. Matchbox would actually become synonymous with die-cast vehicles of any kind.

However, before we explore the exciting era when the Matchbox 1-75 series took hold and changed die-cast collecting forever, let's take a step back in time to the evolution of die-cast model making. After all, while Matchbox has become one of the most popular and instantly recognizable brands in the world, it was far from the first die-cast company.

---

[1] Quotations reprinted with permission of *Collecting Matchbox Diecast Toys: The First Forty Years,* by Kevin McGimpsey and Stewart Orr, 1989.

2 The History That Made Matchbox Possible

Long before Jack Odell made the Coronation Coach and those first Matchbox toys, the history of automotive replicas was born in the same country as the automobile itself: Germany. In the late 1800s, the first automotive toys were constructed in sheet metal, as were the automobiles themselves.

Moses Kohnstam—whose Moko company would become a key to the meteoric growth of Matchbox in the fifties—was developing toy cars in the late nineteenth century. He made clockwork-powered toys crafted of tinplate and, in 1888, he co-founded the Manchester Toy Week, a fair where toy makers could bring their latest inventions.

While the precise date of the first die-cast model isn't known, it appears to have been the brainchild of a German company owned by Ernst Plank. However, Plank's idea didn't catch on until the 1930s when Märklin introduced two series of die-cast automobiles, trucks and military vehicles. During this time, many firms turned to making tin-plate vehicles; the Schuco firm, however, was the largest manufacturer of non-military toys and today is still noted for its ingenious mechanical toys. After the war, Märklin again offered a series of die-cast cars and trucks, as did the firms of Gama and Schuco.

In the 1920s, in France, miniature vehicles were made by three companies and were crafted in iron or tin alloys, and even in plaster and flour. Citröen, the auto manufacturer, issued models of its own cars—both for amusement and promotion—and their extraordinary emphasis on detail forced competing toy manufacturers to improve quality. The other two firms were A. J., which concentrated on Peugot models and C. D., which replicated

Renaults. By the 1930s, companies such as Solido and the French branch of Dinky Toys, as well as C. I. J. and J. R. D., became active in developing die-cast models.

In England, one name gained prominence before the birth of Matchbox: Dinky®. In April 1934, Meccano Ltd., known for its train sets and accompanying miniature accessories, renamed its expanded die-cast model line "Dinky Toys." By the mid thirties, Dinky Toys were firmly established, with some 200 models from the Liverpool plant and many more from the French plant.

As you can see, many companies laid the groundwork for the birth of Matchbox throughout Europe from the late nineteenth to the early twentieth century. But none of these companies captured the attention of children like Matchbox. Matchbox was the first die-cast toy company with a universally recognized brand. And its success began with the famed Matchbox 1-75 series that grew out of those first models developed by Jack Odell.

The Aveling Barford Tractor Shovel

3 The Matchbox 1-75 Series Dominated the Die-Cast Toy World for Decades

The early, small Lesney toys caught fire and became quite a sales sensation, immediately leading to development of the Matchbox 1-75 series. Because of the popularity of the smaller matchbox-size models, the larger toys were phased out by 1954. The Matchbox 1-75 series became one of the most collected, coveted and important collecting phenomena in the twentieth century. It also became one of the most confusing.

Following the early pattern of success (die-cast vehicles performed well, but hardly anything else did), Lesney's early Matchbox 1-75 models were mostly construction and service vehicles. They included the Aveling Barford Road Roller (No. 1), the Muir Hill Site Dumper (No. 2), Cement Mixer (No. 3) and the Massey-Harris Tractor (No. 4). All these miniature models were simply smaller versions of Jack Odell's first models. They were also quite unlike anything the public had ever been exposed to before.

While these Lesney miniatures were the smallest die-cast toys ever developed, they weren't lacking in detail. And, unlike other die-cast toy manufacturers, Matchbox models were often based on the vehicles of the times—the cars, vans, and other vehicles people saw all around them. These replicas appealed to both children and adults, including collectors who prized fine miniatures.

Moreover, "each of the early Lesney toys was packaged in a cardboard box which was printed with a picture of the toy, its name, and in some cases the name of the distributor of the toy— Moko. From a collector's point of view, the toy is more interesting with its original box in good condition, and some have made a science of collecting the boxes."2 Eventually the dual moniker "Moko Lesney" gave way to "Matchbox Cars." This seemed fitting because each Matchbox 1-75 series model came in the familiar small yellow-and-blue box.

Matchbox Was Tough to Beat in Its Combination of Quality and Price

In addition to their small size and high quality, these Matchbox models delivered exceptional value, which goes a long way toward explaining their widespread appeal. With a sticker price of just 7.5p (approximately equivalent to 39 cents), they were affordable to just about everyone, including kids who often went to their local store once a week to buy a new model. Lesney worked hard to keep up with the demand, quickly adding the London Double Decker Bus (No. 5), Quarry Truck (No. 6), Horse-Drawn Milk Float (No. 7), Caterpillar Tractor (No. 8) and Dennis Fire Engine (No. 9). Within just a few years, the range grew to seventy-five models.

In the early sixties, the Matchbox 1-75 series was revamped with some important upgrades. The first was the replacement of metal wheels—which had scratched furniture in homes all over the world—with black or gray plastic wheels. These new models were called "Regular Wheels." The other innovation was glazed windows, which were introduced in 1961. The Matchbox models continued to grow in popularity with annual sales of 100 million models in 1966 and nearly three times as many—286 million models—in 1969. By this time, Matchbox was a global phenomenon with roughly forty percent of total sales being generated in the United States.

A Massey-Harris tractor from 1957, and left, the Aveling Barford Road Roller

The Matchbox 1-75 Series Was Puzzling, Even for Knowledgeable Collectors

Why was the Matchbox 1-75 series so confusing for so many?

As models were added to the series, each received a number. This kept the series current and complete, but collectors had a difficult time following the "logic."

Here's why. "The apparently simple numbering system is actually rather more complex. When models were released, for example, No. 20, the cars produced" bore "no relation to each other. No. 20A was an ERF Heavy Lorry and 20B was an ERF 686 Truck which seems to correspond, but 20C was a Chevrolet Taxi and 20D, a Lamborghini Marzal. This can make collecting difficult as collecting the set, like No.20, means searching for dissimilar models. Should you wish to collect only the trucks and specialize your collection as so many collectors do, then you will also find it difficult, as they appear at almost random intervals in the 1-75 series."[2]

Another reason why Matchbox 1-75 models are so bewildering yet fascinating to collectors is that they were often produced in "variant" models. Frequently, these variants are the ones that command the highest prices when they change hands. How did these variants arise? If the factory ran out of one paint color, it would substitute another. Sometimes variants with a different paint color were produced in extremely small quantities and are therefore highly desirable. For example, "a dark green Morris Minor fetches £30–£40 (USD $45–$60) if in mint condition, but if the car was beige, it can be worth £1,500 (USD $2,220)."[2]

But it's not easy to find these rare models at bargain prices. "Matchbox collectors are known for being knowledgeable about their subject,

meaning that these rare models are constantly being searched for, thus driving up the prices. Even differences in the axle can affect prices. Some collectors have been known to track down every variation of a particular model. A No. 30 Magirus Deutz Crane sold at a specialist auction for a record breaking £7,475 (USD $11,060), all because the jib of the crane was red. The normal silver crane is worth £40–£50 (USD $60–$74) but collectors are willing to pay vast amounts for rarities."

The Matchbox 1-75 series will probably always be an enigma for another reason as well. Berdj Mazmanian, currently Manager of Product Design at Mattel, says, "Nobody knows everything about any given model. There are always legitimate variants turning up that no one knew existed. No one can say with any certainty that all Matchbox 1-75 models are listed or known. Further complicating the picture is the fact that some unscrupulous people will reconstruct a vehicle and try to pass it off as a rare variant."

Variations in color and axles are not the only factors that made some Matchbox 1-75 series models exceedingly more rare than others. Other variations include the style of the wheels, alterations in casting, and the addition or deletion of minor components. Also, around 1960, many of the dies—especially for the earliest models—began to wear out. This is one reason why the number in the series was limited to seventy-five.

Instead of replicating the worn out dies, Lesney decided to issue new models to replace some of the early ones. It became even more difficult for collectors to determine whether they had all the models they needed to keep their collection complete and up-to-date, because the Matchbox 1-75 line had far more than seventy-five models. Many models now had the same number while other numbers had only one model, making the process of collecting the Matchbox 1-75 series both complex and challenging.

Lesney Gains Full Control of Its Trademark and Expands Its Global Reach

In the late fifties, a difference of opinion between Richard Kohnstam and Lesney's management proved fortuitous in more ways than one. The ambitious entrepreneurs at Lesney wanted to expand internationally and were disappointed with Kohnstam's failure to move quickly into foreign markets.

Retailers in South Africa told Lesney that they were only permitted to buy Matchbox models if they also bought other toys offered by J. Kohnstam & Co. Ltd. And, as far as Lesney was concerned, they had launched a successful new series—Models of Yesteryear®—without any help from Richard Kohnstam.

For all these reasons, they decided to buy Kohnstam out of his Matchbox business. They paid him £80,000 for the fifty percent interest in the Matchbox trademark that the Kohnstams had owned since the early fifties, as well as warehouses and offices situated at Clerkenwell Road, City Road and Pentonville Road. One year later, in 1959, Lesney issued its first and second catalogs. "The name Moko was dropped, and by 1961 no longer appeared on the cartons."2

Although the parting of Kohnstam and Lesney was less than amicable, the contribution Richard Kohnstam made to the Lesney legacy cannot be overstated. He had been the marketing arm for Matchbox, credited with the unprecedented success of the Coronation Coach, the development of the Matchbox 1-75 series and Major Packs series that debuted in 1957, as well as gift sets that derived from both the Matchbox 1-75 and Major Packs series. Kohnstam was also the one who brought to Lesney the "Jumbo the Elephant" product concept that helped sustain the company during the lean Korean War years.

In 1959, Fred Bronner was named president of Lesney Products USA. Bronner had been a catalyst in the rapid growth of Matchbox sales in the fifties as the sole importer of Lesney toys into the United States. As the United States became a major market for Lesney, Bronner's stock rose in the company. To recognize Bronner's contributions, Lesney Products (USA) became a major division of Lesney, still headquartered in England. Lesney acquired Fred Bronner's inventory and, subsequently, the Fred Bronner Corporation became the Lesney Products Corporation in the United States.

2 Quotations from *Matchbox Toys,* by Diane and Bruce Stoneback, reprinted with permission of Grange Books.

A Moko Lesney matchbox for a London Trolley Bus

A "Lesney MATCHBOX" for a D-Type Jaguar

Examples of Vehicles from the First Matchbox Series

Cadillac Sixty Special, 1960

Volkswagen 1200 Sedan, 1960

Coca-Cola Lorry, even load, 1956

1958 Vauxhall Cresta, first to have two-tone paint, 1958

Maserati 4CLT Racer, 1958

Bedford Removals Van, 1956

Diesel Road Roller, 1953

Horse-Drawn Milk Float, 1954

Mobile Refreshment Canteen, 1959

Fordson Tractor, first to have rubber tires, 1959

Morris Minor 1000, 1958

Citröen DS19, 1959

Large Long Distance Coach, 1958

ERF Large Road Tanker, ERF 1958

Small Long Distance Coach, 1956

ERF Small Road Tanker, rare green, 1955

The First Matchbox Series

Austin Taxi Cab, 1960

Bedford Evening News Van, 1957

Hillman Minx, rare green, 1958

Ford Thunderbird, 1960

Prime Mover, rare yellow color, 1956

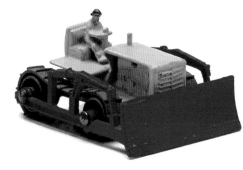

Caterpillar Bulldozer, 1956

Massey-Harris Tractor, 1957

Dennis Fire Escape, 1955

Aston Martin, 1958

Jaguar Sedan, 1959

Ford Thames Van, 1958

Commer Pickup, rare red and white colors, 1958

Dumper, large, 1957

London Bus, large, 1961

Dumper, small, 1953

London Bus, small, 1954

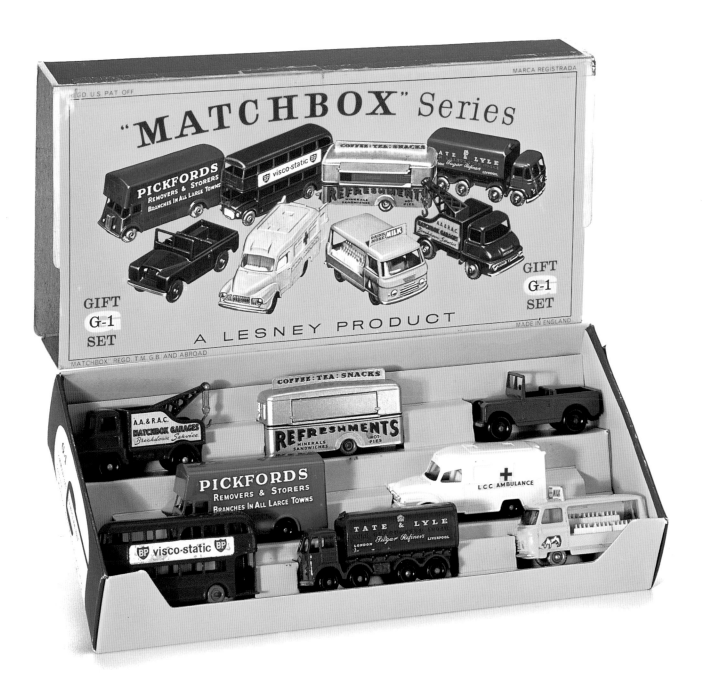

Matchbox Variations

Sharp-eyed Matchbox enthusiasts are always looking for the odd, the different, etc.,

London Trolley Buses, 1958
First bus has red trolley poles and gray wheels.

Second bus has black trolley poles and black wheels.

MATCHBOX Q&A

Q: In what kind of establishment were the first Matchbox toys made?

A: A British public house, commonly known as a "pub."

A-3 Garage, 1957
Jaguar XK120 Coupe, 1957

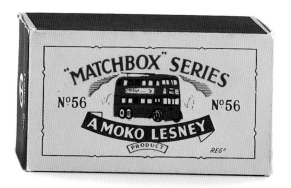

"B" Type Box for the trolley buses on opposite page

Compare the scales and detail between the new and the original double-deckers.

D-Type Jaguar, three models, 1957
First car has dark patch on top of head, with metallic gray wheels that are slightly darker.

Second car has gray plastic wheels.

Third car has red wheels.

"D" Type Box

4 Matchbox Coins a New Term for its Second Major Collecting Series

In 1956, the Matchbox Models of Yesteryear designation was introduced in the desire to create models of vintage vehicles that were more intricately and authentically detailed than anything that had ever been produced in die cast. Jack Odell chose the word "yesteryear," which somehow perfectly describes a series that would also have a lasting impact on the world of die-cast collecting.

Odell said he wanted the Models of Yesteryear range to be a reflection of the past. He had also grown bored with the simpler Matchbox 1-75 series and thirsted for the challenge to make models that were more detailed and intriguing. These fine miniatures depicted antique trucks, buses, and fire engines. They were built in a scale slightly larger than the Matchbox 1-75 series. The Models of Yesteryear series has since become a classic and is very much sought after by collectors today.

The first three models in the Models of Yesteryear series were introduced at the 1956 Toy Trade Fair. The Mettoy company introduced the now famous Corgi line that same year. When Leslie Smith and Jack Odell visited the Mettoy stand at the Harrogate Toy Fair, they were asked to leave. Jack Odell said, ". . . it was the worst thing they could have done as it made us more determined to beat them and turn out cheaper and better stuff."

Because of the tension between the Lesney directors and Richard Kohnstam (over him registering the Matchbox name), Kohnstam was given no part in the Models of Yesteryear launch. A catalog was soon published featuring nine Models of Yesteryear replicas. Within the next thirty years, the series grew. As new Models of Yesteryear were introduced, others were discontinued, adding greatly to their appeal.

To fill the gap left by the ouster of Richard Kohnstam, Lesney hired Peter Webb, who had handled the Matchbox advertising account in his position as Senior Accounts Executive at Dorland Advertising. Webb brought with him both marketing skills and an interest in model railroading. He was instrumental in the continuing success of the Matchbox 1-75, Models of Yesteryear and Major Packs series. And his passion for train collecting was relevant to Matchbox because many Matchbox models were being used in 00 gauge model-train layouts. Webb influenced the number of models crafted to fit the 00 gauge, creating an increasingly stronger bond between model-railroad enthusiasts and Matchbox.

The Evolution of the Models of Yesteryear

Over the years, the packaging has changed with the times. For decades, the packaging included the individual car, the issue number and, of course, the Models of Yesteryear brand name.

Between 1970 and 1972, the Models of Yesteryear series was not produced, although previous models and four-model gift sets were still available. When the series resumed in 1972, older models with new paint jobs were joined by new models based on new tooling. Having bought AMT, a company that made plastic model kits, Matchbox began using more plastic components in the series, particularly in the

1930 Packard Victoria. a giftware model

interiors. Aside from the regularly issued Models of Yesteryear, from 1964 the models were also issued in gold-plated and silver-finished editions attached to pen stands, ashtrays, and other types of presentation gifts.

Sales of Models of Yesteryear vehicles declined through the eighties for a number of reasons. For one thing, an increasing number of competitors were vying for a market that wasn't growing. Some of the competitors were formidable, including Lledo (see Chapter 11). "Also," says Ken Hill, a Mattel senior product designer, "vintage vehicles no longer held strong appeal with consumers who wanted contemporary cars."

The Models of Yesteryear series was based on vehicles manufactured in 1945 or before. This meant that the classic American cars of the fifties and sixties, for example, weren't included in the range. Matchbox Toys had also concluded that the line should be biased toward commercial vehicles rather than automobiles. Not surprisingly, the line appealed to an older, aging market, and not to younger collectors, who preferred Matchbox competitors, including Brumm and Corgi.

By 1983, Models of Yesteryear wasn't selling well and wholesalers began to cut back on their orders. By 1985, collectors were dissatisfied with the high percentage of plastic in the models and concluded that they didn't provide enough value.

In 1985, to try to instill new life into Models of Yesteryear, Matchbox broke with tradition and issued a four-model set of sixties-era race cars. Unfortunately, however, the models were deemed to have too much plastic and they failed. Then Matchbox contemplated a new range. While this initiative was never realized, Matchbox did develop a die-cast model of the 1955 BMW 507 V8 Roadster, a car owned by Elvis Presley. This "orphan" model was eventually incorporated into Models of Yesteryear.

Also slated for launch in 1987 was a replica of the E-Type Jaguar. The plan was to fold this

1967 Jaguar E-Type MK 1-1/2

replica into Models of Yesteryear, as well, and make it the range's 1988 Special Limited Edition. This was about the time that Matchbox was contemplating the acquisition of Dinky, in part to add new life to a declining enterprise (see Chapter 10).

In the early nineties, just when it seemed that Models of Yesteryear might be a dying brand, along came Matchbox Collectibles to the rescue. This new direct-marketing arm began offering thematic series and more intricate and highly detailed models, many with the Models of Yesteryear brand. Often reflecting advances in die-cast engineering and innovative model-making techniques, these models sold quite well through the end of the decade. These recent editions continued the Models of Yesteryear tradition of capturing the cars that were the most popular or significant designs of their era.

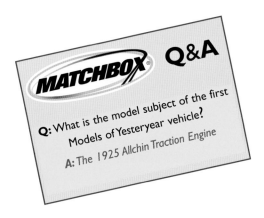

MATCHBOX® Q&A

Q: What is the model subject of the first Models of Yesteryear vehicle?

A: The 1925 Allchin Traction Engine

Early Models of Yesteryear Vehicles

1925 Allchin Traction Engine, with very rare rear wheels

1911 London "B" Type Bus, Dewar's

1918 Leyland Four-Ton Van, Jacob's, with very rare missing center line of text

1926 Morris Cowley Bullnose Car

MATCHBOX® Q&A

Q: What was the first version second No. 1 Models of Yesteryear vehicle? What was its color and what makes it rare?
A: A red Model T Ford, with a twin brake lever

1826 "General" Class Locomotive, Santa Fe, in very rare mid green

1907 London "E" Class Tramcar, *News of the World*

1924 Fowler "Big Lion" Showman's Engine, with rare gold cylinder block

1914 Sunbeam Motorcycle with Milford Sidecar in very rare gold finish

1929 Bentley Le Mans, with rare gray folded-down hood

1903 "Duke of Connaught" Locomotove, with scarce gold sandboxes

MATCHBOX Q&A

Q: Which Models of Yesteryear vehicle was the first to feature solid wheels?
A: The YY7 Leyland Van introduced in 1957

Early Models of Yesteryear Vehicles

1920 Aveling & Porter Steam Roller,
with rare gold makers plate

1899 London Horse-Drawn Bus, Lipton's Tea

1916 AEC "Y" Type Lorry, Osram Lamps, in
exceptionally rare light blue

1928 Sentinel Steam Lorry, Sand & Gravel,
with rare plastic wheels

MATCHBOX Q&A

Q: Which three colors were used for
the Models of Yesteryear Unic Taxi?
A: Red, blue, and white

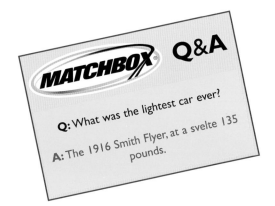

MATCHBOX Q&A

Q: What was the lightest car ever?
A: The 1916 Smith Flyer, at a svelte 135
pounds.

By 1968, vehicles from the early twentieth century dominated the selection.

Matchbox in the Sixties

Ford Refuse Truck, 1966

Dodge Cattle Truck, 1966

Dodge Wreck Truck, 1965

Dodge Wreck Truck,
rare reverse colors, 1965

Leyland Royal Tiger Coach, 1961

Mercedes-Benz 300SE, 1968

John Deere Tractor, 1964

Lotus Racing Car, 1966

Chevy Impala
with Sports Boat
and Trailer, 1961

Ford Cortina, 1968

Safari Land Rover, 1965

Volkswagen Camper, 1962

Fordson Tractor

Caterpillar Bulldozer, 1964

Mercury Cougar, 1968

Mercedes-Benz 300SE, 1968

Ferrari F-1 Racing Car, 1962

Rolls Royce Phantom V, 1964

Chevrolet Impala Taxi, rare gray wheels, 1965

Jaguar XKE, 1962

Matchbox in the Sixties

Field Car, green wheels (rare variation), 1969

TV Service Van, 1963

Pipe Truck, 1966

Sugar Container Truck, 1961

Ford GT, 1965

Iso Grifo, 1968

Volkswagen 1500 Saloon, 1968

Ford Fairlane Fire Chief Car, 1963

Ford Anglia, 1961

Pontiac Convertible, 1962

Claas Combine Harvester, 1967

Dodge Cattle Truck, 1966

Dodge Dumper Truck, 1966

Petrol Tanker, 1964

Mercedes-Benz Ambulance, 1968

Aveling Barford
Tractor Shovel, 1962

MG1100, 1966

Ferrari Berlinetta, rare red color, 1965

Jeep Gladiator Pickup, rare green interior, 1964

Road Roller, 1958

Matchbox Military Models

Volkswagen Dormobile Ambulance, 1970

Scammell Breakdown Truck, 1959

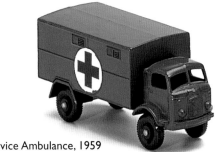

Ford Service Ambulance, 1959

Ferret Scout Car, 1959

Saracen Personnel Carrier, 1958

Unimog, 1970

Weasel, 1974

Austin MKII Radio Truck, 1959

D.U.K.W., 1958

General Service Lorry, 1959

Self-Propelled Gun, 1976

M3 Personnel Carrier, 1958

Saladin Armored Car, 1959

Swamp Rat, 1976

Land Rover, 1959

Alvis Stalwart, 1966

M-Z Bradley Tank, 1998

Ten-Ton Pressure Refueller, 1959

M3 Thornycroft Antar and Centurion Tank (Major Pack)

41

A Matchbox Garage (in reverse colors, a rare variation), red garage and yellow base, 1957; shown with a 1962 Jaguar XKE and a 1958 Ford Thames Van

A 1963 Fire Station; shown with a Fire Chief's Car and a Merryweather Marquis Fire Engine.

5 Matchbox Goes Big with the Major Packs and King Size Series

Introduced in 1957, Major Packs represented a new range for Lesney. Although crafted to the same scale as the Matchbox 1-75 miniatures, they were larger models, which gave Lesney an entrée into new markets. The first model in the series was the Caterpillar DW20 Earth Scraper.

Over a decade, some fifteen models were produced before the series was abandoned. Frankly, Lesney didn't seem to know quite what to do with the series. As a result, while some of the models were continued in the King Size range, Major Packs was discontinued in 1967.

Several years after the introduction of Major Packs, Lesney unveiled the mighty King Size series.

A Major Pack GMC Tractor and Freuhof Hopper Train; also seen as King Size

A Car Transporter from the Accessory Series: It carried six regular Matchbox vehicles.

Interstate Double Freighter

Pickford's 200-Ton Transporter

A pre-production King Size Airport Crash Tender, never released. It was fashioned after a Corgi model of this casting that was released. This model could actually pump water.

King Size Articulated Horse Box, Ascot Stables, 1967

King Size Racing Transporter, 1967

King Size Models

Tractor Transporter, with three "orange" tractors
(making the model rare)

DAF Car Transporter

Merryweather Fire Engine

Prime Mover, with a rare label
on the trailer

Dodge Tractor with Twin Tippers

Pipe Truck

6 A Tax Problem Leads to a Decade of Explosive Growth

In 1956, Lesney's accountant told the directors they should spend a lot of money on something, anything, to avoid paying excessive taxes. Even though the company didn't feel that building a new factory was necessary, that's how they spent the money. At 59 Eastway, Hackney Wick, London, the new factory easily accommodated "eighty machines and a workforce of over one thousand."

Benjamin Franklin once quipped that there are only two things certain in life, and one of them is taxes. He might have added that tax problems don't go away for prosperous enterprises like Lesney Products as it prepared itself for the psychedelic decade of the 1960s. The company decided to go public, issuing some 400,000 shares of stock, which were quickly oversubscribed.

Why did Lesney go public after more than a decade of rapid growth and profitability as a private company? Jack Odell said the decision was made because the tax laws favored a public company and Lesney was about to get hit with a big tax liability. According to *Collecting Matchbox Diecast Toys: The First Forty Years* by Kevin McGimpsey and Stewart Orr, the *Times of London* gave this assessment of the company as it began issuing stock: "About 80% of the Lesney production is devoted to small toys . . . over half the output is exported to more than ninety overseas territories. The remaining 20% of the business is in small light commercial diecasting," which was Lesney's original focus way back in 1947.

The *Times* also reported that Lesney's new factory would be paid for from existing funds, not from the capital generated through the stock offering, which was no doubt attractive to investors.

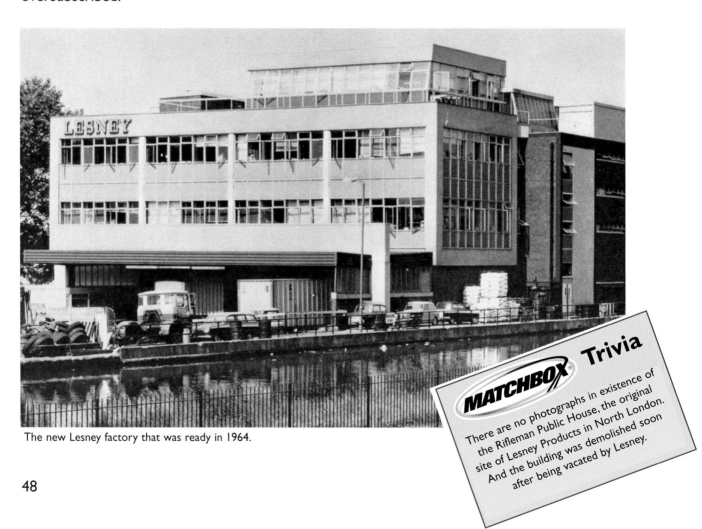

The new Lesney factory that was ready in 1964.

MATCHBOX Trivia

There are no photographs in existence of the Rifleman Public House, the original site of Lesney Products in North London. And the building was demolished soon after being vacated by Lesney.

Another new London factory awaits machinery in 1967.

Lesney Enjoys Unprecedented Success and Prestige in the Sixties

Lesney didn't miss a beat in the sixties. Both sales and accolades multiplied over and over. One reason for the company's success is that it was still very well positioned with respect to its competition. Companies like Corgi and Dinky sold higher-priced models, which generally required the consumer to make a premeditated decision to go to a toy shop to make the acquisition. Lesney models, on the other hand, were still very inexpensive and were sold in many high-traffic destinations—such as gift shops, department stores, and even newsstands and post offices. As a result, Matchbox models were often bought on impulse, requiring little thought.

When Lesney was honored with its first Queen's Award to Industry, the company employed more than 3,600 people and was manufacturing 100 million models annually. The company's 1966 catalog said that if one year's models were placed together in a line, they would stretch from London to Mexico City, a distance of roughly 6,000 miles. During 1967 and 1968, Lesney's sales were 28 million pounds and five million profit, earning the company a place in the *Guiness Book of Records* as the

The Matchbox design and development office

49

company with the highest profit "with capital employed than any other company in England." Other milestones during this exciting decade for Lesney included:

- Construction of a new factory of over 100,000 square feet in Edmonton in 1967. Among other things, the facility housed fourteen double-decker buses that were used to transport employees. Nearly twenty percent of the factory was used for production of "Matchbox Motorway." This was a plastic track with a spring that would propel a Matchbox 1-75 model forward and down the track. (Although initial sales were very good, the Motorway quickly faded.)

- Leslie Smith and Jack Odell received Order of the British Empire (O.B.E.) awards. Lesney Products garnered its second Queen's Award to Industry.

- Chosen by the chairman of the Smithsonian Institution, a total of twenty-one Matchbox models were sealed in four time capsules. One was opened in 1993; the others will be opened in 2018, 2068, and 2968.

- By the end of the decade, Lesney had fourteen factories, employed well over 6,000 people, and received its third Queen's Award to Industry. In 1969, the Queen visited the Lesney factories at Hackney, accompanied by the Duke of Edinburgh.

Although the sixties was in many ways the most glorious decade in Lesney's history and the company was confident about its future prospects, storm clouds began to appear on the horizon. For the first time in nearly forty years, the company would get its first taste of serious competition. And the impact is still being felt to this very day.

MATCHBOX Trivia

On a single afternoon in 1961, Matchbox made more Rolls-Royce Silver Ghosts than Rolls-Royce Ltd. had produced in sixty years.

50

Some of the die-casting machines designed by Jack Odell

The automatic spraying machines traversed backwards and forwards across a moving belt of models, giving them three coats of lead-free paint.

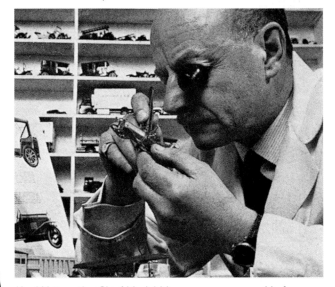

Ken Wetton, the Chief Model Manager, was responsible for many of the models during the sixties and seventies.

G-5 Gift Sets being packaged. They are now worth over $105 each.

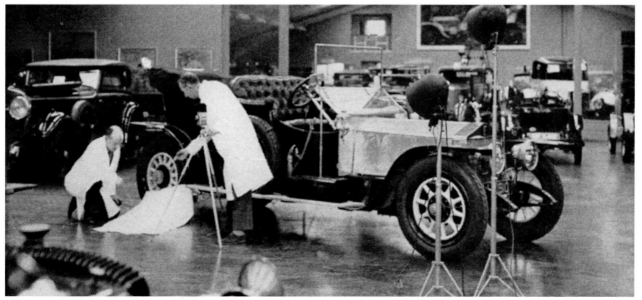

A 1907 Rolls-Royce is accurately measured to ensure
its true scale miniaturization as a Model of Yesteryear vehicle.

7 Matchbox Responds to a Major Threat

A great irony arose when Mattel acquired Tyco in 1996 and took possession of the Matchbox brand. The company whose Hot Wheels® models nearly sank Matchbox in the late sixties now had both powerful die-cast trademarks under the same roof.

For over twenty years, Matchbox had increased its sales and its worldwide reach without any significant threat from a competitor. Then, in 1968, Mattel introduced "Hot Wheels" with a $10 million advertising campaign, which was a very substantial sum to be invested in a single campaign back then. But it wasn't only the clever advertising that commanded consumers' attention. It was also the special qualities these new Hot Wheels die-cast toys had to offer.

Hot Wheels frictionless wheels made them much faster on a track, giving them far superior play value. The impact was immediate and devastating: Matchbox sales in the U.S. plummeted from $28 million to $6 million. Many say Lesney was slow to react, but their response came in the second half of 1969 when they introduced their new "SuperFast" models. Within a couple of years, much of the Matchbox 1-75 range was converted into SuperFast.

What specifically did Lesney do to react to the Hot Wheels threat? The new models were equipped with thinner axles, new wheels and bold paint schemes, making them fast and exciting enough to compete with Hot Wheels.

Hot Wheels was mainly an American phenomenon, whereas Matchbox was far more international. However, Hot Wheels had a dramatic impact on Lesney and its successor companies. For many years, Matchbox and Hot Wheels sales volumes were comparable, more or less running neck and neck. But then, in the mid-1990s, Hot Wheels started pulling away from Matchbox and soon became the best selling die-cast brand. Fortunately, by then, both brands were owned by the same company: Mattel.

But, nearly three decades before the Hot Wheels and Matchbox brands were under the same corporate roof, the decade that began with such promise for Lesney and Matchbox—the sixties—ended with uncertainty. In addition to suddenly having a formidable competitor, Lesney had other problems. Hot Wheels was one of a number of competitors who were manufacturing models in China and the Far East where labor costs were substantially lower than the United Kingdom, placing enormous pressure on Lesney.

And yet, the company somehow managed to control its own destiny for another decade or so, despite a series of setbacks.

See page 77 to spot the variations of this 1970 Beach Buggy model.

Spot the Difference between these three 1975 Fandangos

The first car has blue fan, purple windows, "35" label.

The second car has chrome fan, clear windows, "35" label.

The third car has blue fan, clear windows, sunburst label. It is the rarest of these models. The label was actually issued on another model.

The SuperFast Models

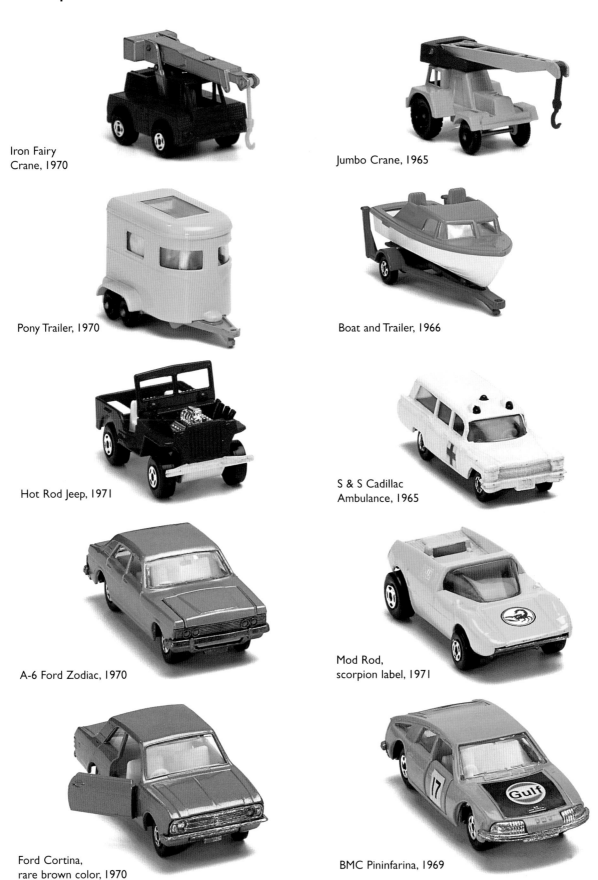

Iron Fairy
Crane, 1970

Jumbo Crane, 1965

Pony Trailer, 1970

Boat and Trailer, 1966

Hot Rod Jeep, 1971

S & S Cadillac
Ambulance, 1965

A-6 Ford Zodiac, 1970

Mod Rod,
scorpion label, 1971

Ford Cortina,
rare brown color, 1970

BMC Pininfarina, 1969

Volkswagen Camper, raised roof, 1967

Volkswagen Camper, 1968

Mercedes-Benz 500SL Convertible, 1990

Field Car, Military, 1970

Turbo Fury, scorpion label, 1973

Blue Shark, scorpion label, 1971

Ford GT, rare yellow, limited issue, 1970

Dodge Charger, rare Castrol, label, 1970

Ford Group 6 Racer, in rare non-metallic green, 1970

Ford Group 6 Racer, 1970

The SuperFast Models

Mack Dump Truck, 1970

Honda Motorcycle and Trailer, 1970

Mercury Cougar Dragster, 1970

Hary Hustler, scorpion label, 1971

Lamborghini Miura, rare yellow color, 1969

Merryweather Fire Engine, one of the first promotional models/boxes produced by Matchbox, 1978

Ford Pickup, 1970

Dodge Dragster, rare version, label not proper for model, 1971

Porsche 910, scorpion label, 1970

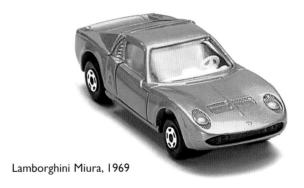

Lamborghini Miura, 1969

Trailer Caravan, 1965

Field Car,
rare white color, 1970

Road Dragster,
scorpion label, 1970

Mercedes 230SL, 1970

Setra Coach, 1970

Greyhound Bus, tinted yellow windows, 1970

Mercedes
Ambulance, 1970

Pontiac Grand Prix
Sports Coupe, 1970

Ford Mustang, rare red color, red interior, 1970

Rolls-Royce
Silver Shadow Coupe, 1969

Lesney Giftware Models

Produced by Lesney Industries for mounting on a variety of wooden bookends, boxes, and porcelain dishes and ashtrays, these models from the 1970s and early 1980s were finished in either a gold- or bright-silver-effect vacuum-plating,

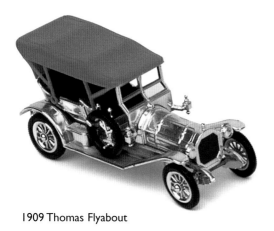

1909 Thomas Flyabout

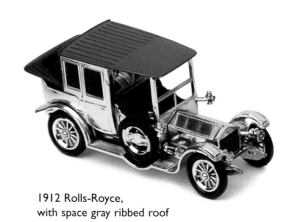

1912 Rolls-Royce,
with space gray ribbed roof

1930 Packard Victoria

1904 Spyker Veteran Automobile

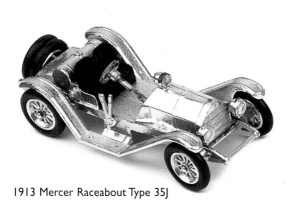

1913 Mercer Raceabout Type 35J

1911 Renault Two-Seater

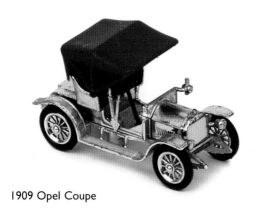

1909 Opel Coupe

1918 Crossley Truck Ambulance,
with rare rear canopy

1911 Daimler Type A12

1907 Rolls-Royce Silver Ghost

1928 Mercedes-Benz 36-220

1914 "Prince Henry" Vauxhall

Lesney Giftware Models

1911 Ford Model T Car, with scarce red plastics

1918 Crossley Truck Coals and Coke Delivery Vehicle

1929 Bentley Le Mans

1907 Rolls-Royce Silver Ghost

1911 Maxwell Roadster

1934 Riley MPH (always with painted fenders)

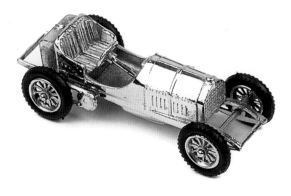

1908 Mercedes "Grand Prix" Racer, very rare issue

1926 Bugatti Type 35, rare issue

Models of Yesteryear Vehicles from the Sixties

1911 Ford Model T Car,
with rare black textured roof

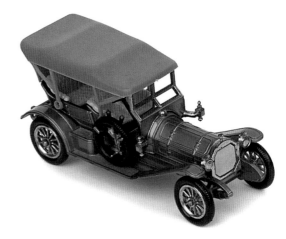

1909 Thomas Flyabout,
with very rare yellow seats and grille

1938 Lagonda Drophead Coupe, with extremely
rare purple fenders

1928 Mercedes-Benz SS Coupe,
with scarce "Stutz" green fenders

1912 Packard Landaulet

1914 Prince Henry Vauxhall, with rare orange body

1930 Deusenberg Model "J" Town Car, with rare green roof and tan seats

1907 Peugot, in yellow with rare gold roof

1930 Packard Victoria, in gold, with extremely rare black fenders

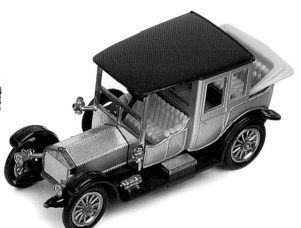

1912 Rolls-Royce, with exceptionally rare yellow seats

1910 Benz Limousine, in rare dark green and chartreuse livery

1909 Opel Coupe, with rare maroon seats and grille

Models of Yesteryear Vehicles from the Sixties

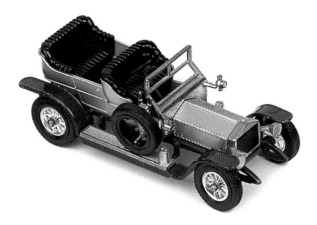

1906 Rolls-Royce Silver Ghost, in silver,
with very rare purple-red fenders

1931 Stutz Bearcat

1904 Spyker Veteran Automobile,
in extremely rare maroon livery

1928 Mercedes-Benz,
with extremely rare black seats

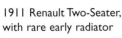

1911 Renault Two-Seater,
with rare early radiator

1913 Cadillac,
with scarce textured roof

1945 MG, "TC," with scarce red wheels

1912 Simplex

1934 Riley MPH,
in very rare purple with black seats

1926 Bugatti Type 35, with rare gray tires

1913 Mercer Raceabout,
with rare gray tires

1929 Bentley 4-1/2 Liter, in rare apple-green livery

1936 Jaguar SS100: the first truly classic sports car produced by
Jaguar is captured perfectly in miniature by Lesney in 1977.

1936 Jaguar SS100: the only Models of Yesteryear vehicle
produced entirely in pewter.

1938 Lagonda Drophead Coupe: an extremely rare issue, with gold body and purple chassis/fenders, this is one of the most desirable Models of Yesteryear.

1930 Deusenberg Model "J" Town Car: the most famous Models of Yesteryear issue of all time and arguably the best "classic" in the range. The livery of white body and red chassis/fenders was originally rejected as "too toy-like," and only a couple of dozen or so escaped being scrapped.

The SuperFast Grand Prix Track, 1971,
with Red Road Dragster and Blue Piston Popper

8 Matchbox Zigs and Zags through the Seventies

Before the introduction of Hot Wheels impacted Lesney, the company was doing just fine. Lesney was crafting over five million models every week and exporting to 130 countries—including the United States, which accounted for forty percent of exports. In 1970, Lesney received its fourth Queen's Award to Industry in five years. Moreover, Lesney was truly a global enterprise and this advantage would help the company survive the seventies.

Also, the SuperFast line got off to a fast start. By 1971, Lesney was producing over six million SuperFast models per week. To strengthen the link between SuperFast and racing, Lesney became the proud sponsor of a Formula Two race car. The Matchbox car was driven by four-time World Motorcycling Champion and by former World Racing Champion John Surtees and nine-time World Motorcycling Champion Mike Hailwood. Lesney figured that their primary market—kids—would be more enthusiastic about Superfast models now that Matchbox was involved in world-class racing.

At about this same time, Lesney also began to diversify aggressively into other toy categories. The company began offering plastic kits in 1971, which were costly yet profitable. During the following year, Lesney introduced its first product outside the automotive model arena. Called "Cascade," it was a family game that featured steel balls that were propelled over "thumper drums." In 1973, Lesney unveiled "Rola-matics." These models were equipped with components that moved as the model's wheels rolled.

Toward the end of 1975, Lesney invested heavily in promoting "Fighting Furies," a series of action dolls that were jointed so they could be posed in various ways. This product line also included an adventure ship and a carrying case that doubled as a bridge and the deck of a Spanish galleon. Lesney also introduced the "Disco" girls and, in

1977, acquired Vogue Dolls from Tonka; so the company was clearly in the doll business. Lesney's acquisition of Vogue Dolls was a particularly shrewd move. Vogue was in poor shape, and Lesney bought it for what was said to be a very low price. Lesney revamped the doll line and it quickly became a winning enterprise.

By 1977, Lesney was producing an ever-expanding array of toys for boys and girls.

Two Strikes: a Fire, and a Flood Hit Lesney in the Seventies

All these new product launches came on the heels of a series of business and financial setbacks. The money drain that ultimately crippled Lesney can be traced back to the threat that Hot Wheels represented. For nearly two years, Lesney had to invest a great deal of human and financial capital to change tooling and production for the SuperFast models. The financial resources built through the sixties began to dwindle and Lesney started losing money.

Just as one might conclude that Lesney Products had been remarkably lucky for the first twenty years of its existence, its fortunes would change for the worse in the seventies. Jack Odell resigned in 1973, leaving Lesney Smith to manage a troubled company by himself. Then there were two strikes in quick succession. The first—a national power strike that lasted eight agonizing weeks—shut down production at Lesney. This was followed by a strike at one of Lesney's plants. Finally, a fire ravaged the company's Rochford factory, destroying most of the valuable plastic components. Then the banks of a nearby river overflowed, flooding the already decimated plant and rendering the surviving machinery inoperable.

As a result of these disasters, Lesney obviously had limited production capability. So they shut down production of Models of Yesteryear vehicles for roughly two years, giving their hot-selling

SuperFast line top priority. The Models of Yesteryear series wasn't revived until 1975.

Although Lesney was still making acquisitions in the late seventies, they didn't all work out for the best. In 1978, Lesney Products bought AMT, an American company that made plastic model kits, a business Lesney was developing. However, AMT suffered a series of problems, including difficulties in relocating the company from Detroit to Baltimore, which adversely impacted production. When Lesney fell into receivership in 1982, AMT was acquired by Ertl.

Packaging: In Some Ways, It's Almost as Important as the Model

As knowledgeable collectors know, a model in its original packaging—preferably unopened—is often far more desirable than the model alone. But the packaging itself has been the subject of serious analysis because of its impact on cost and, of course, the price the consumer pays. In other words, packaging cost affects how competitive the pricing can be.

All through Matchbox history, packaging has been a subject of concern, whether the brand was owned by Lesney, Universal, Tyco, or Mattel. And the issue has been especially important for the Matchbox 1-75 miniature line. Should models be packaged in closed boxes, window boxes, or blister cards—and what is the optimum size?

In the late seventies, Lesney stopped using closed boxes and used small and large blister packs instead. The idea was to let customers in each market determine which type of packaging they preferred. Certain markets wanted blisters because they were cheaper than window boxes, but others wanted the same "footprint" as a window box. That's how the so-called blister card came about.

In the eighties and through much of the nineties, a small blister pack was about half the price of a large blister pack, which cost about

the same as a closed box. And a window box cost about double a large blister. So, as you can see, the cost differentials were significant, as were the ultimate prices at retail.

A detail showing part of a blister pack from the eighties

For the past two decades or so, Matchbox packaging has been affected by many factors, including the varying perspectives of internal marketing executives and the ascendancy or decline of sales and profits in a given market. To this day, many markets around the world still feel that every Matchbox model should be in a box to preserve the tradition of the original matchbox-size models. But, when packaging can account for twenty-five percent of the product price, one has to weigh preference against practicality.

Ultimately, the consumer or collector can hold sway. For example, in the mid-nineties, The managers of matchbox Collectibles decided to replace the decorative boxes with the simple, functional packaging that other direct-marketing die-cast—collectibles use. After all, it's far cheaper. However, the collectors reacted vehemently, and the marketers reversed course and used printed packaging once again.

Hence, while easily overlooked, packaging has always played an important role in the collectibility, perceived value, and price of Matchbox models.

Models from Matchbox MBI–75, As They Enter Their Third Decade

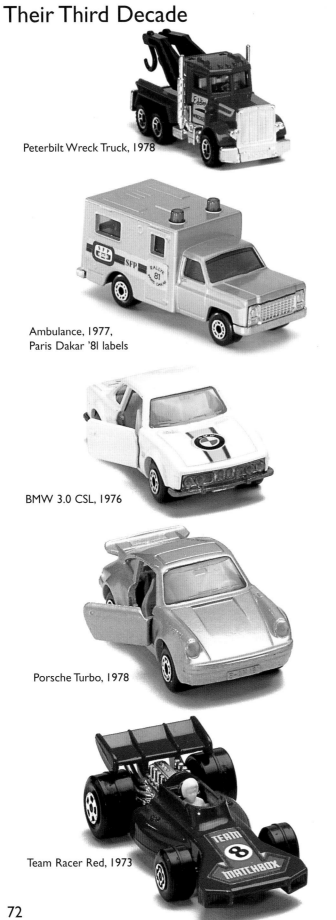

Peterbilt Wreck Truck, 1978

Ambulance, 1977,
Paris Dakar '81 labels

BMW 3.0 CSL, 1976

Porsche Turbo, 1978

Team Racer Red, 1973

Armored Truck,
1978

Tractor Shovel,
1976

Citröen S.M., 1972

VW Golf, 1976

Police Motorcycle, 1977

DAF Girder Truck, 1970

Scaffold Truck, 1970

Chop Suey, 1973, rare chrome handlebars

Airport Coach, 1977

Dodge Challenger 1976

AMX Javelin 1972

Renault STL Le Car, 1978

Seafire, 1975

Formula 5000, 1975

Chevrolet Corvette, 1979

Models from Matchbox MB1–75, As They Enter Their Third Decade

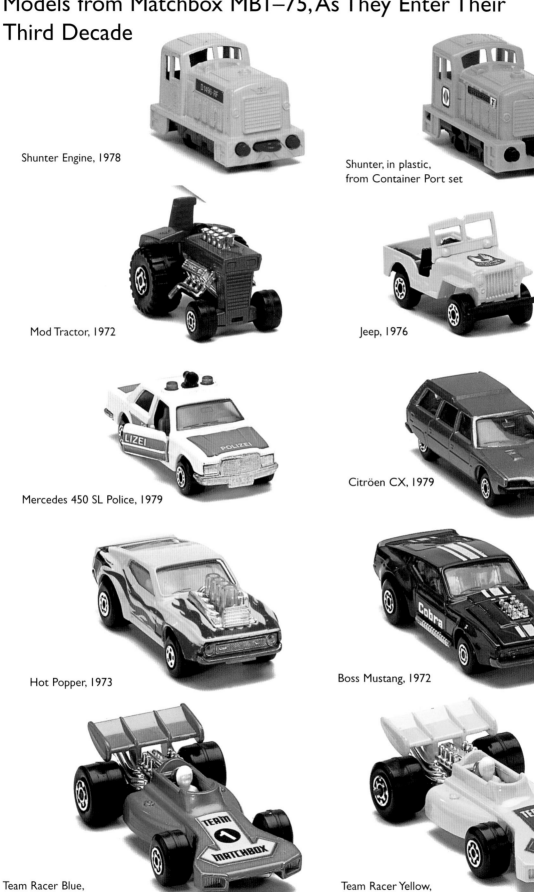

Shunter Engine, 1978

Shunter, in plastic, from Container Port set

Mod Tractor, 1972

Jeep, 1976

Mercedes 450 SL Police, 1979

Citröen CX, 1979

Hot Popper, 1973

Boss Mustang, 1972

Team Racer Blue, only available in View-Master set

Team Racer Yellow, only available in View-Master set

Mercedes Container Truck, 1977

Freeway Gas Tanker, 1973, and
Freeway Gas Trailer, 1973

Tow Joe, 1972,
rare hitchhiker
labels

Airport Coach, 1977

Rallye Royal, 1981

Seasprite Helicopter, 1977

Plymouth Grand Fury Police Car, 1979

Rolls-Royce Silver Shadow II, 1979

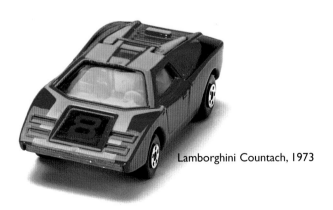

Lamborghini Countach, 1973

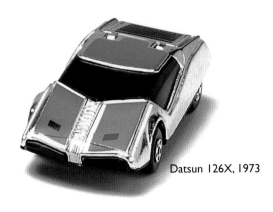

Datsun 126X, 1973

Spot the Difference

Three Car Transporters, 1976:
The first transporter has medium blue car on bottom.

The second transporter has dark blue car on bottom.

The third transporter has lighter blue car on bottom
and has black wheels.

Two Sports Boats and Trailers, 1961:
The first boat has a silver engine,
and the first trailer has gray wheels.

The second boat has a gold engine,
and the second trailer has black wheels.

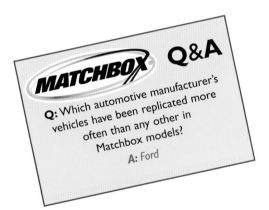

MATCHBOX Q&A

Q: Which automotive manufacturer's
vehicles have been replicated more
often than any other in
Matchbox models?
A: Ford

Three Beach Buggies, 1970:
The first car is darkest, with least speckling, and a white bottom.

The second car has a pale purple roof and a yellow bottom.

The third car has most speckling and a yellow bottom.

Examples
of
Packaging

TP-4 HOLIDAY SET

Package: Vauxhall Guildsman
and Eccles Caravan

Military King Size Pack
Armored Car Transporter,
foreign-issue in dark
olive color

Package: Ford Tractor and Hay Trailer

MM2-A Armored Car Transporter

Car Ferry, 1977

Safari Land Rover, on ramp; Volkswagen Camper and Field Car, on ferry;
Iso Griffo and Iron Fairy Crane, front of ferry

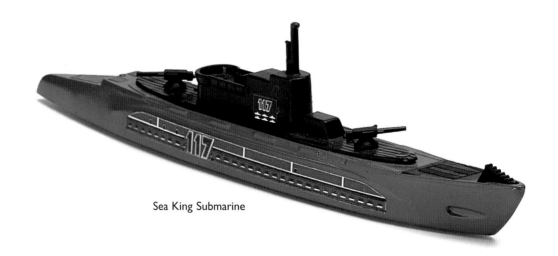

Sea King Submarine

Sea Kings

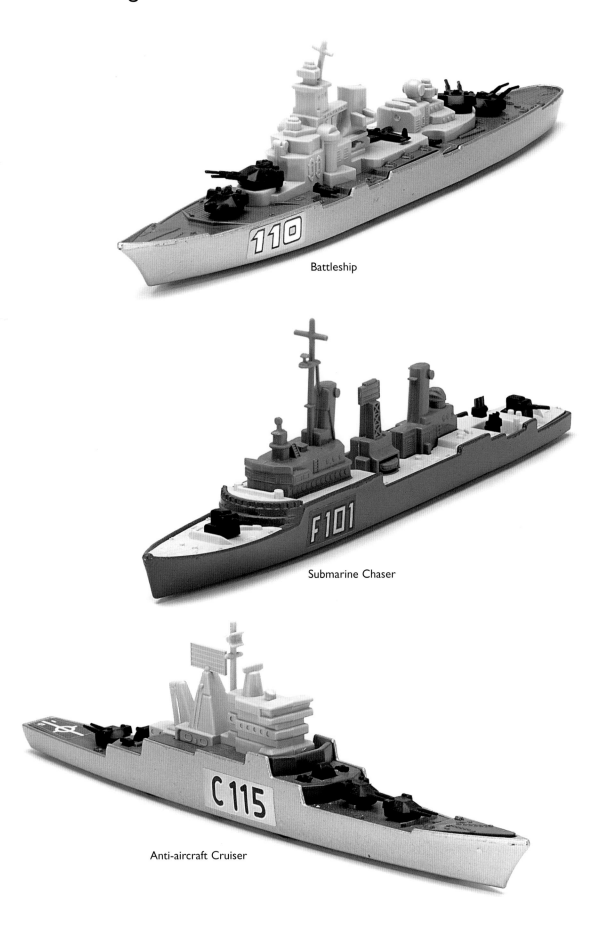

Battleship

Submarine Chaser

Anti-aircraft Cruiser

81

9 Matchbox Rises from the Ashes and Regains Momentum

In 1980, Lesney lost 3.6 million pounds due to weak demand for its products and a strong pound. The company's financial woes were aggravated by a British recession. Lesney was soon forced to seek bank loans. Jack Odell was coaxed out of retirement and appointed vice chairman in the hope that he could repair the leaky ship.

But, in this same year, the wheels were already in motion for the first acquisition of a company that had enjoyed much prosperity and had suffered considerable adversity since its birth decades before. For it was in 1980 that David Yeh initiated discussions with Leslie Smith and Jack Odell to manufacture Lesney products in Yeh's Far East factory. One of the first new product introductions to be made in Yeh's facilities was a series of Disney characters, which met with instant success. The Goofy character is particularly sought after as a collectible.

David Yeh had been critical of Lesney Products' high costs of producing product in its factories in the United Kingdom, and he certainly had a point. In addition to far higher labor costs, Lesney had to pay export duties, especially when shipping product to the United States. However, initially at least, the shift to producing Matchbox models in Asia didn't seem to help. In fact, manufacturing there ceased, a decision attributed to high manufacturing costs, especially in Japan.

Yeh also felt that Lesney wasn't keeping up with the American market. American kids were often buying competitors' models of American cars instead of the Lesney Matchbox line, which was heavily skewed toward British and other European cars.

Lesney Products Changes Hands for the Very First Time and Becomes Matchbox International

"In 1982 Lesney had a workforce of 3,500 and had six operating plants within the United Kingdom as well as over 500 employees and several operations in twelve other countries." And, by the early days of 1982, Lesney's operating loss exceeded $15 million. The company's creditors were losing patience. On June 11, 1982, perhaps the darkest day in Lesney history, the company was declared bankrupt and ushered into receivership.

Even before then, Lesney had begun to discuss the sale of the company with various parties. Ironically, Mattel, which now owns the Matchbox brand, was among the suitors, as was Fisher-Price, which is now owned by Mattel as well. Most of Lesney Products' assets were transferred to a shell company called Matchbox Toys Ltd., and this entity was purchased out of receivership by David Yeh's Universal Toys, based in Hong Kong.

Not surprisingly, Universal decided to make Matchbox models in its Macau facilities, where labor was far cheaper than in England. There was one notable exception: Models of Yesteryear vehicles continued to be crafted in Rochford, England, until 1985, at which time production of this famous series was also switched to the Macau factories.

David Yeh's Ambition Fuels an International Die-Cast Juggernaut

In addition to the manufacturing arrangement that David Yeh had with Lesney, there were other earlier developments that help explain Yeh's interest in—and ultimate acquisition of—Lesney Products. In 1955, he began working for the Louis Marx Company in Hong Kong. This is where he received an early education in the toy business directly from the principal of the company, Louis Marx. Marx told Yeh about Matchbox, and the company developed a line of plastic models similar in size and style to the Matchbox die-cast replicas.

In 1964, David Yeh invested $10,000 of his own savings in Universal Doll Dress and Universal Traders. Using leased sewing machines, the company made dresses for dolls. Then, in 1967, he bought Modern Diecasting, changing its name to Universal Diecasting. He also founded Universal Manufacturers Ltd., which crafted wooden toys in Taiwan. The Universal Group began manufacturing plastic toys in 1971 and, a year later, consolidated its marketing and manufacturing operations under one umbrella called Universal International Holdings.

Seeking to expand business in the U.S. market, The Universal Group created Kidco Toys in 1977 as the U.S. marketing arm of Universal Toys. In 1978, Universal bought most of LJN Toys, a small American toy importer and distributor based in New York. After Universal acquired Lesney, the Kidco and LJN product lines were marketed under the Matchbox brand in Europe. In 1980, Universal took over 100,000 square feet of factory space and formed Macau Toys Ltd. And, in 1981, Universal created Macau Diecasting Toys Ltd.

What all these developments reveal is a consistent pattern. Over a period of many years, David Yeh continually expanded his toy business and moved specifically into die-cast manufacturing, which made his acquisition of Lesney Products a natural evolution of his desire to keep growing. Universal doubled in size when it bought Lesney. And David Yeh was ecstatic. Yeh's offer was 16.5 million pounds and, although the purchase price wasn't revealed, he characterized it as "the bargain of the century."

In 1983, Matchbox International was formed. And, for the time being, the future of Matchbox looked rosy again. Three years after the purchase of Lesney, Matchbox made a handsome profit of $6 million. In 1986, Matchbox Toys was declared the best-selling line in Europe, and the toys were sold in 120 countries. In that same year, Universal Matchbox reported net sales of $257 million, with nearly $17 million in profits.

By 1988, the company had over 5,000 employees with four manufacturing facilities. Three were in the Far East in Hong Kong, Macau and China. And one remained in the United Kingdom. This plant in Rochford, Essex, continued producing the highly profitable plastic model kits, as well as preschool products. Apparently it was actually cheaper to keep this type of manufacturing in England because of the cost of shipping bulky items from Asia.

But the Far East was still very important to The Universal Group and David Yeh, for he believed that China represented a huge untapped market for his toys. The company began a dialog with financial and cultural institutions in China and announced that a collection of Matchbox models would be placed on permanent display at the Children's Palace in Shanghai in 1989.

Incidentally, in that same year, 1989, Matchbox senior product designer Ken Hill created an innovative new line called "World Class." He had seen Hot Wheels models with rubberlike tires, and his "World Class" series became the first Matchbox models equipped with them. The models also featured individually crafted headlights and taillights, as well as messages on license plates. The series required a more complex crafting process than previous Matchbox series, including vacuum metallized windows and silver molded wheels.

Ken Hill was beginning to advance the art and science of die-cast model-making, creating models that were more like fine collectibles than toys. He was setting the stage for Matchbox Collectibles, which would begin producing replicas in the nineties geared to the adult collector.

Sky Busters

Boeing Stearman

Piper Comanche

Spitfire

A-300 B Airbus

Boeing 747-400

Cessna Float Plane

Cessna 210 US Army: a pre-production trial, it was never issued as U.S. Army.

Junkers

Boeing 777-200

Boeing 747-400

Grumman F-14 Tomcat

Tornado

Mig 21

Harrier

MATCHBOX Q&A

Q: What is unusual about the SB010, 747-100 in the Nippon Airways livery?
A: It was only sold in the Japanese Airport set of 1988.

Tornado

NASA Space Shuttle

RAF Harrier

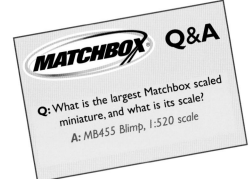

F117 Stealth Fighter

Two Examples of Interactive Matchbox Vehicles

Convoy Grove Crane, 1992

King Size Snorkel Fire Truck, 1980:
This model had a retractable stabilizer to hold the
vehicle steady while the Simon Snorkel Hydraulic
Platform was raised.

Military Models, Issued through the Seventies to Nineties

Mercedes Truck and Trailer, 1970

Field Gun, 1978

Badger, 1974

Freeway Gas Tanker,
rare French flag, 1973

Stoat, 1974

M4A3 Sherman Tank, 1999

Police Patrol Ambulance,
chrome hubs, not regular issue, 1975

Field Car, 1970

Ford Expedition, 1999

Hummer, 1994

Rocket Transporter, 1990

Jeep, 1976

M1A1 Abrams Tank, 1995

Jeep, chrome hubs not normal issue, 1976

M1A1 Abrams Tank, 1995

Jeep, 1976

M1A1 Abrams Tank, 1995

Mission Helicopter, 1985

Models of Yesteryear: The "Commercial Explosion"

1930 Ford Model A Van, OXO, with rare red interior

Ford Model A Van, Toblerone

1912 Ford Model T Van "Motor 100,"
with very rare reverse colors on globe

1930 Ford Model A Wrecker,
Barlows, a rare Macau issue

1918 Crossley Truck
R.A.F. Ambulance,
with rare burgundy seats

1927 Talbot Van, Lipton's Tea, City Road

1930 Leyland Titan Bus, Southdown

1937 GMC Van, Goblin, with scarce gray roof

1930 Ford Model A Woody Wagon

1929 Morris Cowley Light Van, Michelin

1917 Yorkshire Steam Lorry, Johnnie Walker Whisky

1912 Ford Model T Van, Coca-Cola,
with very rare five vertical coach lines

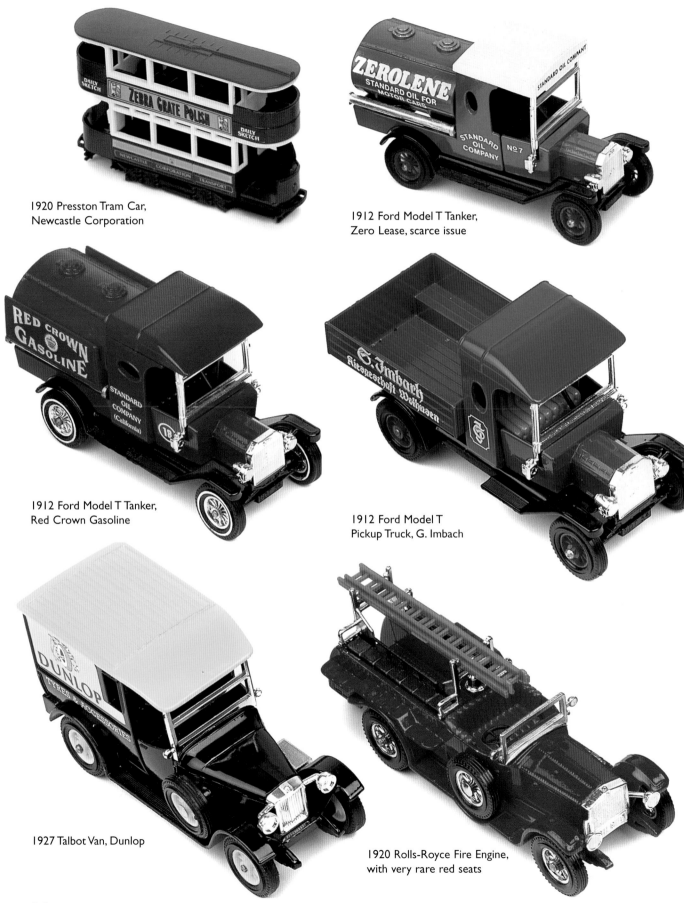

1920 Presston Tram Car,
Newcastle Corporation

1912 Ford Model T Tanker,
Zero Lease, scarce issue

1912 Ford Model T Tanker,
Red Crown Gasoline

1912 Ford Model T
Pickup Truck, G. Imbach

1927 Talbot Van, Dunlop

1920 Rolls-Royce Fire Engine,
with very rare red seats

1926 Ford TT Van, Drambuie

1930 Ford Model A Woody Van, A&J Box

1918 Crossley Truck, Carlsberg, with rare ice blue canopies

1927 Talbot Van, Nestle's, with rare black roof

1918 Atkinson Steam Lorry, Lake Goldsmith

1912 Ford Model T Van, Birds Custard, in scarce metallic blue

King Size Models: Seventies and Eighties

ERF Snorkel Fire Engine, 1980

Fire Engine, 1984

Tank Transporter (Battle King)

Fire Tender, 1973

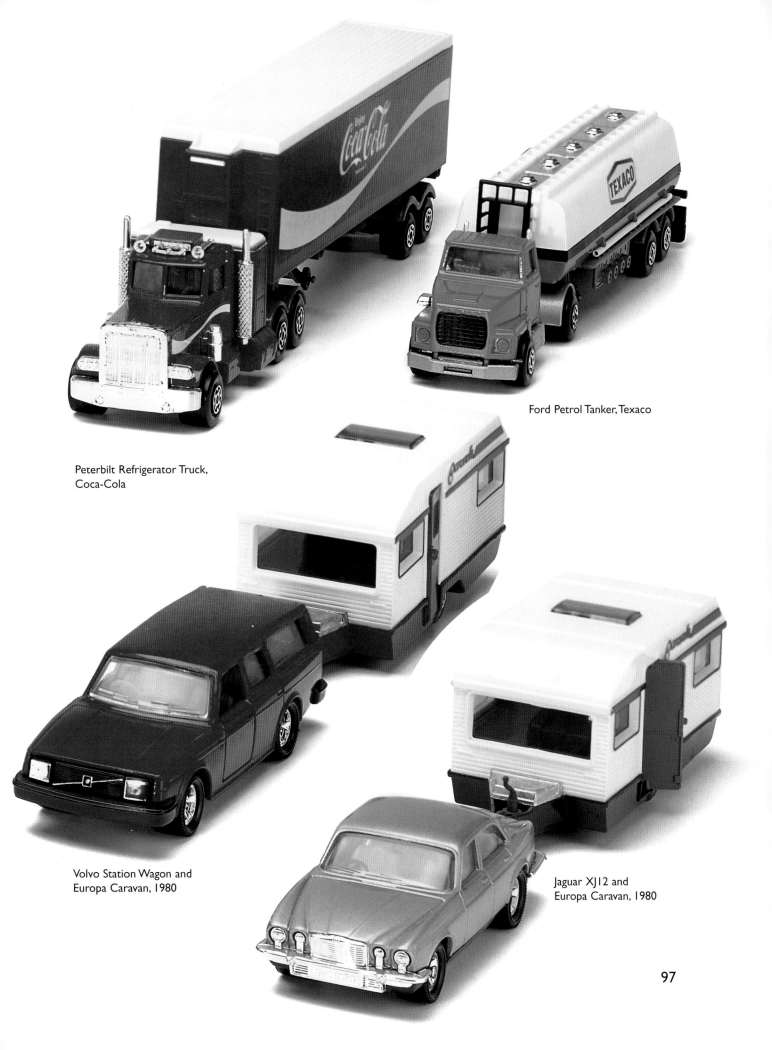

Peterbilt Refrigerator Truck,
Coca-Cola

Ford Petrol Tanker, Texaco

Volvo Station Wagon and
Europa Caravan, 1980

Jaguar XJ12 and
Europa Caravan, 1980

97

Matchbox 38s: Based on the Ford Model A Van

BBC

Kellogg's Rice Krispies

Johnsons Seeds

Matchbox, with China labels, very rare

Streets Ice Cream

Rowntree's Table Jelly

A Unique Models of Yesteryear Vehicle

1912 Ford Model T Van, Taystee Bread, 1980:
The Taystee logo was applied to just a few hundred Ford T Vans,
instead of the 1927 Talbot Van, and thus was created the rarest Ford
Model T Van in the range.

MATCHBOX Trivia

In May 1993, a 1904 Spyler from the
Models of Yesteryear series sold for £1,800
to a German collector.

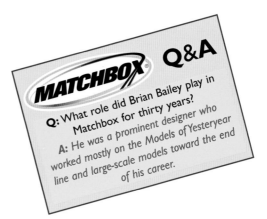

MATCHBOX Q&A

Q: What role did Brian Bailey play in
Matchbox for thirty years?
A: He was a prominent designer who
worked mostly on the Models of Yesteryear
line and large-scale models toward the end
of his career.

Matchbox SuperFast Models

Peterbilt Quarry
Truck, 1982

Ford Transit
Ambulance, 1986

Blaze Buster Fire
Truck, rare white
ladder, 1975

Ikarus Bus, 1986

Jeep Cherokee,
1986

Jeep Cherokee, 1986

Porsche 944
Turbo, 1984

Greased Lightning, 1983

Mercedes G Wagon and Horse Trailer, 1970

Land Rover 90, 1986

Volvo Tilt Truck, 1984

Volvo Zoo Truck, 1982

Matra Rancho, 1982

4x4 Jeep, 1982

Mercedes-Benz
300SE, 1986

Mercury Sable
Wagon, 1987

Jaguar SS100, 1982

Jaguar SS100, 1982

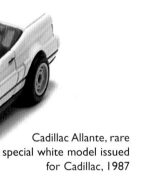

Cadillac Allante, rare
special white model issued
for Cadillac, 1987

Pontiac Firebird, 1979

Matchbox SuperFast Models

Extending Ladder
Fire Truck, 1984

Dodge Caravan, 1984

Audi Quatro, 1982

Pontiac Firebird SE, 1982

Boss Mustang, 1982

Midnight Magic, 1981

Datsun 240Z, 1981

Toyota Supura, 1983

Porsche 928, 1980

Porsche 928, 1980

Volvo Container Truck, 1985

Volvo Cable Truck, 1982

Cement Truck, 1982

Helicopter, 1982

1987 Corvette, 1987

London Taxi, 1987

Citröen 15CV, 1983

Ford Sierra XR4I, 1983

1957 Ford Thunderbird, 1982

Ford T-Bird Turbo Coupe,
1987

King Size resin production of the Viper Morehead Car for the TV show *Viper*, along with blister card package never released; car has working parts

Pre-production Experiments

Dodge Stealth (casting designed on scale of a
slot car and was rejected by Chrysler)

White Tractor

1972 Cadillac Ambulance, hand trial, never issued

Green Hornet, never issued

Bugatti

1965 GTO Pontiac, never issued

Convoy Models from the Eighties and Beyond

DAF Racing Transporter, Ferrari

DAF Boat Transporter, Coast Guard

Scania Tanker, Amoco Gas

Container Truck, Firestone

DAF Box Fire Truck, Pirelli

Ford Aeromax Box Truck, Albertsons

DAF Boat Transporter

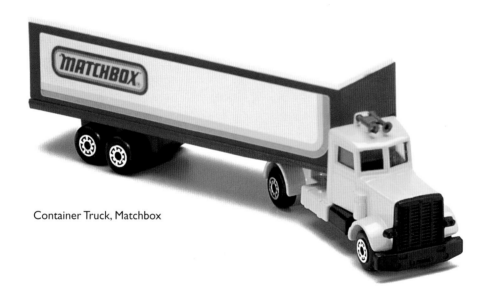

Container Truck, Matchbox

DAF Box Fire Truck, World Cup Soccer

Peterbilt Gas Tanker, Getty

Bigger Is Better

1937 GMC Van, Steinlager: The brand owners objected to the size of the logo on the right-hand model, which was reduced to the left-hand model. But some of the "large logo" Steinlager models were mistakenly distributed, thus creating another "classic" collectible.

MATCHBOX Trivia

The town of Budweis, because of its royal brewery, called its lager "the Beer of Kings." In our day, Anheuser-Busch calls their Budweiser beer "the King of Beers."

Matchbox Convoy Models

Scania Box Truck, Saudia Airlines

Scania Box Truck, Heinz

Scania Covered Truck, Michelin

Mack Box Truck, FedEx

Scania

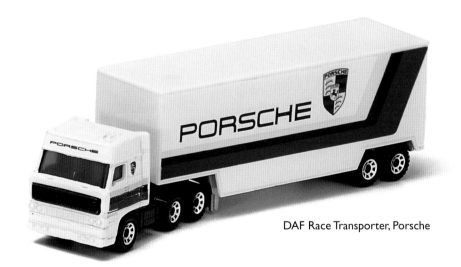

DAF Race Transporter, Porsche

113

Grove Crane:
See it demonstrated on page 88.

Peterbilt Lowboy and Bulldozer

Peterbilt Tanker, Arco, premiere

Kenworth T-2000 Box Truck, premiere

MATCHBOX® Q&A

Q: The Convoy Horse Transporter tool was modified to create which vehicle?

A: The Matchbox NASA Tracking vehicle

Scania Tanker, Shell

Mack Box Truck, Mack Trucks

Box Truck, Skittles

Kenworth

Kenworth Box Truck, Kellogg's Corn Flakes

Kenworth Double Container Truck, Pepsi,
rare, hard to find issue with Pepsi labels

Matchbox Convoy Models

Kenworth C.O.E. Container Truck, Mayflower

Ford Box Truck, Goodyear

MATCHBOX® Trivia

In 1932, while recuperating from an operation, Mack's chief engineer, Alfred Fellows Masury, carved the Mack bulldog. This was the beginning of one of the world's most recognized symbols.

Kenworth Box Truck, Harley-Davidson

Kenworth Box Truck, K-Line,
limited issue done for K-Line in special packaging

MATCHBOX® **Q&A**

Q: What is a tampo machine, and where was the process first patented?
A: The tampo machine was patented in Germany. It is the process whereby inks are transferred from a container onto a surface for decoration.

Laser Wheels

Ford Sierra XR4i
with tnted windows

Ford Sierra XR4i

Camaro Z-28

Camaro Z-28

Nissan 300ZX

Buick LeSabre Race Car

Ford Escort Cabriolet

Volvo 480ES

Racing Porsche

Chevy Pro Stocker Race Car

Corvette

Corvette

Pontiac Firebird Racer

Pontiac Firebird Racer

T-Bird Turbo Coupe

Mercury Police Car

Toyota MR2 Pace Car

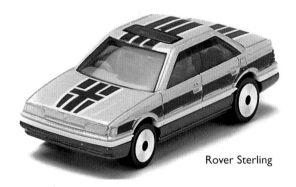

Rover Sterling

Peugot Quasar

Pontiac Fiero

Laser Wheels

AMG Mercedes 500 SEC with black headlights

AMG Mercedes 500 SEC with gray headlights

Datsun 280ZX
with gray finish

Datsun 280ZX
with black finish

BMW 323 Cabriolet

Lamborghini Countach

Ferrari 308 GBT

Saab 9000

Cadillac Allante

1962 Corvette

Corvette with roll bar

Corvette

Ferrari Testarossa with gray finish

Ferrari Testarossa

Porshe 928 with light blue strip on door

Porshe 928

Porshe 928 with added lettering on roof

Dodge Daytona

Pontiac Firebird SE

Sauber Group C Racer

Privately Commissioned Models of Yesteryear

1912 Ford Model T Van,
Ronald McDonald House,
Australia

1929 Garrett Steam Lorry,
Pickfords

1931 Morris Pantechnicon,
Classic Toys Magazine

1922 Foden Steam Lorry,
MICA

1948 Dodge Route
Van, Express Delivery

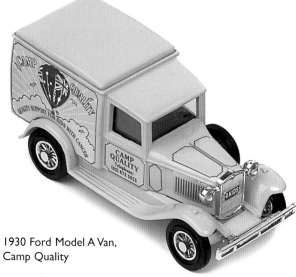

1930 Ford Model A Van,
Camp Quality

1931 Morris Pantechnicon, Ronald
McDonald House,
Victoria, Australia

1937 GMC Van, Cessnock
Rescue Squad, Australia

1905 Fowler B6
Showmans Engine, Billy Smarts

1926 Ford Model TT Van,
Matchbox USA

1932 Mercedes-Benz L5 Lorry, Ronald McDonald
House, Queensland, Australia

1937 GMC Van, Chester Toy and Doll Museum

Privately Commissioned Models of Yesteryear

1939 Bedford Tanker,
Belrose, Australia, Bush Fire Brigade

1926 Ford Model TT Van,
Matchbox USA

1894 Aveling & Porter Steam
Roller, F. Dibnah & Son

1952 Land Rover and Trailer,
Londonderry, Australia,
Fire Brigade

1912 Ford Model T Van,
Matchbox Junior Collectors Club

1922 Foden Steam Lorry,
Fullers Brewery

1929 Garrett Steam Lorry, Chester Mystery Plays

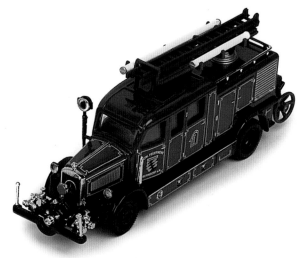

1938 Mercedes-Benz KS15 Fire Truck, Obendorf

1929 Morris Light Van,
R.S.P.C.A.

1955 Holden FJ/2104 Panel Van,
Auto One

1955 Holden FJ/2104 Panel Van,
Temora District Ambulance

1932 Mercedes-Benz
Ladder (Fire) Truck,
Solingen-Berg

1929 Scammel 100-Ton Low Loader and G.E.R. E4 Class 2-4-0 Locomotive:
The largest Models of Yesteryear ever and the first time this particular locomotive
had ever been mass produced.

1930 Ahrens Fox Quad Fire Engine: The longest fire engine of its era
perfectly miniaturized by Matchbox Collectibles for inclusion in
the Models of Yesteryear range.

Two Long Models of Yesteryear

MATCHBOX Trivia

The lowest priced mass-produced American car was the 1925 Ford Model T Runabout: $260.

MATCHBOX Q&A

Q: Which four liveries or decorations have appeared on the little known Walker Electric Van in the Models of Yesteryear series?

A: Harrods Ltd; Joseph Lucas; HMV in blue and Harrods Bread

10 The Dinky-Matchbox Connection

Although the Dinky Toys name was not used until April of 1934, actual Dinky Toys models were on the market as early as the latter part of 1933. At that point, they were known as Modelled Miniatures and were produced by Frank Hornby's legendary Meccano company, a firm most noted for its electric trains.

Dinky Toys cars and trucks were initially intended to be accessories for train sets. These miniature cars added realism to the miniature towns, farms and country settings through which electric trains coursed. Some 1934 Dinky Toys models included a Town Sedan, a Vogue Saloon, a Super Streamline Saloon, a Sportsman Coupe, a Four-Seater Tourer and a Two-Seater Tourer. All were priced at just nine shillings, except for the Town Sedan, which sold for a pound.

Almost immediately after their introduction, Dinky Toys vehicles were being produced in Liverpool, England, and Bobigny, France, beginning a unique relationship between the Dinky Toys of the two nations. Although British Dinky and French Dinky seldom used the same models, they did create series that were related in theme. With great success in two separate, non-competing markets, there seemed to be nothing that could hold Dinky Toys back. Nothing, that is, except for the onslaught of World War II.

As the war unfolded, Dinky Toys halted production—with its thirty-eight series of sports cars only half completed. New models would not be produced until 1946, although the 1945 Christmas season saw Dinky Toys selling prewar models to meet the seasonal demand.

Dinky Toys Changed by the War

The postwar years saw subtle changes incorporated in the models. Rubber was scarce, so French Dinky switched to all-metal wheels; at the same time, British Dinky began using cast, raised hubs on its wheels. Also, at the same time, Dinky began expanding its line. Dinky Supertoys was introduced in 1947, featuring larger models with treaded tires and die-cast wheel hubs. Among the Supertoys were such models as the Foden Eight-Wheel High-Side Truck and a Foden eight-wheeled fourteen-ton Tanker. Other trucks in the regular Dinky Toys line were equipped with cargo beds that tipped backward. By the 1950s, the Dinky catalog had grown to such proportions that the numbering system in both the French and British systems was changed. (The British Dinky Toys were re-numbered from 1954 to 1956 and the French Dinky Toys were re-numbered in 1959.)

Dinky Captures the Excitement of the Fifties

The fifties were marked by increased competition in the die-cast market. Corgi Toys had made an auspicious debut and Dinky responded by developing plastic windows and suspensions and bright two-toned color finishes. Another offshoot, Dublo Dinky Toys, appeared in 1956 and was intended to be used on 00 gauge railroad platforms. The line never really took off and was withdrawn before the end of the decade. But throughout the fifties, Dinky became more exacting in its attention to detail; finishes seemed brighter and models reflected the buoyancy of the times.

Advertising on the sides of Dinky models became more common. While Dinky had made trucks with familiar brand names such as Oxo Beef in Brief, Wakefields Castrol Motor Oil, Firestone Tyres, and Marsh's Sausages in the early days, the advertisements on the fifties-models seemed bolder and brighter. Mobilgas, EssoPetroleum and Shell/BP marked the sides of tankers; Lyons Swiss Rolls and Weetabix were elegantly placed on Guy vans; and Raleigh Cycles, Ovaltine, Kodak, Royal Mail, and even Dinky Toys appeared on the sides of Austin,

Bedford, and Morris vans, respectively. In fact, like the advertisements in real life, those that appeared on Dinky Toys models became more graphic and vivid with each coming year.

Bigger Is Better in the Turbulent Sixties

When Dinky Toys was bought by Tri-Ang in 1963, Dinky had just issued its first antique car. Soon business was expanded and the first models were produced in Hong Kong. Later, Hong Kong produced Mini-Dinky Toys that came packed in their own garage. The sixties also saw Dinky produce larger scale models, moving from 1:43 to 1:35, as well as finger-tip steering.

Die-cast model design in the sixties was also influenced by the success of Mattel's Hot Wheels. Soon Dinky Toys and many other manufacturers followed suit with their own versions of souped-up, surrealistic vehicles. For Dinky, these were dubbed Dinky Speedwheels. Cartoon and outer space characters, TV stars and other figures appeared on many of the Dinky Toy vehicles.

Dinky Falls, Rises, and Joins the Matchbox Family

The next decade was rather dire for Dinky Toys. The French firm ceased production in 1972, and the British branch folded in 1980. Other companies, including Pilen, Solido, Polistil and Universal, attempted to keep up the manufacture of particular Dinky Toys, but the effort was short-lived.

In 1987, the Dinky Toys name was sold to Universal International. This was a perfect wedding between two of the major die-cast manufacturers and brought Dinky and Matchbox together as members of the same corporate family. At the same time, other companies bought old Dinky Toys dies. A firm in India, which had bought the dies early, marketed its models as Nicky Toys; Polistil bought some of the last dies; and some dies made their way to South America.

At the time of the Universal acquisition, Dinky belonged to another toy company, Kenner-Parker. Reportedly, the sale price was a real steal. The fact that Dinky seemed to be a bargain was no doubt a major impetus for the acquisition.

Matchbox also apparently feared that another major toy company might move on Dinky, such as Corgi or Lledo. Even though Kenner-Parker hadn't produced the brand for nearly a decade, Dinky was still surprisingly well recognized. In fact, people within Matchbox considered Dinky stronger than Models of Yesteryear and almost as well known as Matchbox itself.

Aside from its bargain price, Dinky was no doubt acquired for strategic reasons as well. While the name Models of Yesteryear was associated with replicas of prewar vehicles, Dinky had been known for postwar designs. And, while Matchbox was very inconsistent with scale—generally making models within each range of roughly the same size and, therefore, of wildly different scales—Dinky had always adhered to the 1:43 scale. With Dinky under the Universal umbrella, the company could maintain the integrity of Models of Yesteryear while using Dinky to exploit markets that weren't being served adequately.

Because Dinky had been neglected for so long by Kenner-Parker, there weren't any production molds to use for models. So the first series from Matchbox to bear the Dinky trademark consisted of three Matchbox models in blister packs. This represents another interesting irony: the earliest Matchbox models were based on Dinky models; yet, when Matchbox acquired Dinky, the first Dinky models were actually Matchbox. "The first Dinky prototypes were shown at the Harrogate Toy Fair in January 1988."[1]

1955 B61 Tractor-Trailer, McDonalds

1939 Triumph Dolomite

1955 Bentley "R" Type Continental

1953 Austin A40 Van, Dinky Toys

1948 Commer 8cwt. Van, Sharp's Toffee

1950 Mercedes-Benz
Konferenz Type O-3500 Bus

1957 Chevrolet Bel Air, Hot Rod

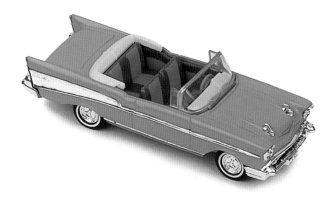

1957 Chevrolet Bel Air Convertible,
with scarce brown seats

1953 Buick Skylark Convertible

1973 Ferrari Dino 246 GTS

1968 Volkswagen Karmann-Ghia Convertible

The Return of Dinky Toys (Manufactured by Matchbox)

1958 Buick Special Convertible

1946 Delahaye 145 Chapron

1948 Land Rover, A.A.

1967 Jaguar E-Type MK 1-1/2,
the first model in the range

1957 Citröen 2CV

1998 Volkswagen Concept 1 Convertible

1959 Cadillac Coupe De Ville

1957 Studebaker Golden Hawk

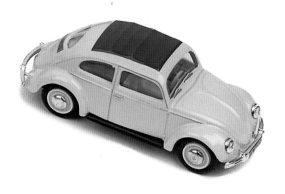

1951 Volkswagen Beetle De Luxe Sedan

1965 Triumph TR4A-IRS

1961 Lotus Super 7, the rarest Dinky of all

1964 Austin Mini, Cooper S

1952 Citröen 15CV: A truly classic postwar French car that successfully pioneered front-wheel drive and a "fluid" suspension.

MATCHBOX Trivia

For a period immediately following World War II, Citröen offered its automobiles to the French market in matte black only.

MATCHBOX Trivia

A widely believed but false story was that Citröen was named after the shape of the DS21, which looked like a lemon (Citröen is French for lemon).

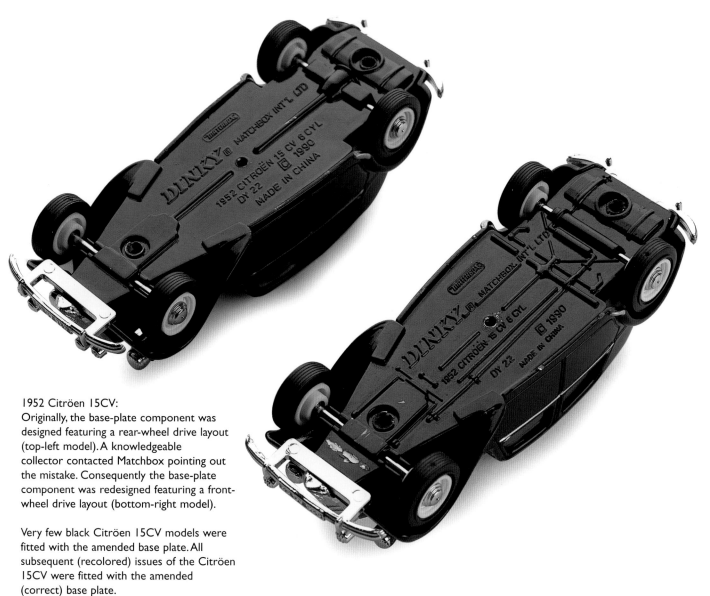

1952 Citröen 15CV:
Originally, the base-plate component was designed featuring a rear-wheel drive layout (top-left model). A knowledgeable collector contacted Matchbox pointing out the mistake. Consequently the base-plate component was redesigned featuring a front-wheel drive layout (bottom-right model).

Very few black Citröen 15CV models were fitted with the amended base plate. All subsequent (recolored) issues of the Citröen 15CV were fitted with the amended (correct) base plate.

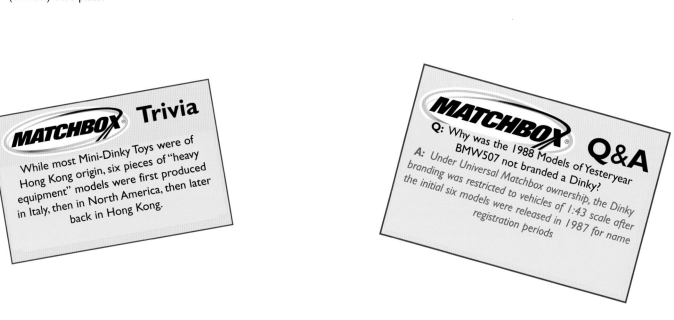

MATCHBOX Trivia

While most Mini-Dinky Toys were of Hong Kong origin, six pieces of "heavy equipment" models were first produced in Italy, then in North America, then later back in Hong Kong.

MATCHBOX Q&A

Q: Why was the 1988 Models of Yesteryear BMW507 not branded a Dinky?
A: Under Universal Matchbox ownership, the Dinky branding was restricted to vehicles of 1:43 scale after the initial six models were released in 1987 for name registration periods

1967 Series 1-1/2 E-Type Jaguar: The only Matchbox Dinky model cast entirely in pewter.

The Lledo-Matchbox Connection

After Universal bought Lesney in 1982, Jack Odell purchased a considerable amount of the company's tooling and die-cast machinery and formed a company called Lledo. Once again—just as in the case of Lesney and Moko—the company name was very personal.

During World War II, while serving in the African desert, Jack Odell knew it would be very dangerous if he forgot his radio call sign, so he made it "Lledo," which is Odell spelled backwards. And, just as Lesney was formed by two old chums, so was Lledo. Jack Odell set up his new company in concert with Bert Russell, a friend of his from the earlier days of making Matchbox models.

The two entrepreneurs figured they would focus on making a limited number of larger scale models. The first six produced were called the "Days Gone" series, which consisted of five horse-drawn vehicles and a van based on the Ford Model T. Odell and Russell were trying to create a turn-of-the century feel to appeal to the collector's affinity for nostalgia. This introductory series showed up on store shelves in 1983.

Lledo also began producing what are known in collector circles as "promotional models," bearing company logos, slogans, and other graphics. These models were often used as gifts to customers, giveaways at conferences and shows, and special promotions, including new product launches. The first model offered was the same Model T van from the Days Gone series, which continued to be produced as a promotional model for many companies. In fact, over the years, millions of Model Ts were decorated with corporate graphics, creating a continuous source of income for Lledo.

1912 Ford Model T Van, U.S. Mail

Recognizing the strength of the promotional models market, Lledo made a substantial investment in die-cast tooling for another seven models, this time based on vehicles from the twenties and thirties. Once again, these models were sold to the public as the Days Gone series and were customized as promotional models for companies. This dual income stream gave Lledo the capital it needed to continually invest in new tooling and keep expanding the line. Lledo attracted an enthusiastic following of collectors and began introducing themed sets. The first, in 1987, was a set of three models depicting vintage airfield support vehicles and was issued to honor the 75th anniversary of the Royal Flying Corps in a limited edition of 10,000. This new dimension was highly successful for Lledo and spurred development of subsequent limited-edition commemorative sets.

Other milestones in Lledo history include the first individual model to generate over £1 million in sales. It was issued in 1989 with a portion of the proceeds benefiting the RAF Benevolent Fund. Lledo began a collector club that same year and soon had thousands of members throughout the world. In 1993, the company launched an important new series called "Days Gone Vanguards," featuring models based on vehicles from the fifties and sixties, which have also been popular among collectors. And, in 1996, based on research, the company began developing more authentic and detailed replicas, which were also distinguished by the fact that they were still crafted in the United Kingdom.

Lledo became the biggest die-cast company still manufacturing in Great Britain and the largest producer of promotional models in the country. And, like Matchbox, Lledo models are still collected the world over.

In 1996, Lledo was acquired by the HCG group (the acronym stands for Hobbies, Collectibles, Gifts), which makes dolls, sports collectibles, medallions and other products. Shortly after the acquisition, Bert Russell retired. Jack Odell became Life President. Then, in 1999, Lledo was acquired by Corgi, another die-cast company whose history is intertwined with that of Matchbox.

1910 Renault Ambulance, British Red Cross

1926 Ford Model TT Van, Pro Hart, a quantity of 1,000 was issued

Models of Yesteryear

1907 UNIC Taxi

1933 Cadillac 452 V16

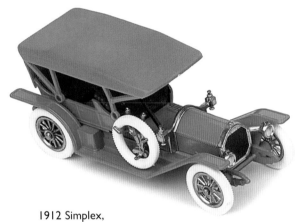

1912 Simplex,
with trial white tires

1913 Cadillac,
with trial white tires

1937 Mercedes-Benz 540K

1938 Lincoln Zephyr

1930 Bugatti Royale Napoleon

1928 Bugatti T44

1928 Mercedes-Benz SS Coupe with extremely
rare white body and black fenders

1911 Ford Model T, with trial white tires

1971 Plymouth Cuba 44

1937 Cord 812 Sedan

Models of Yesteryear

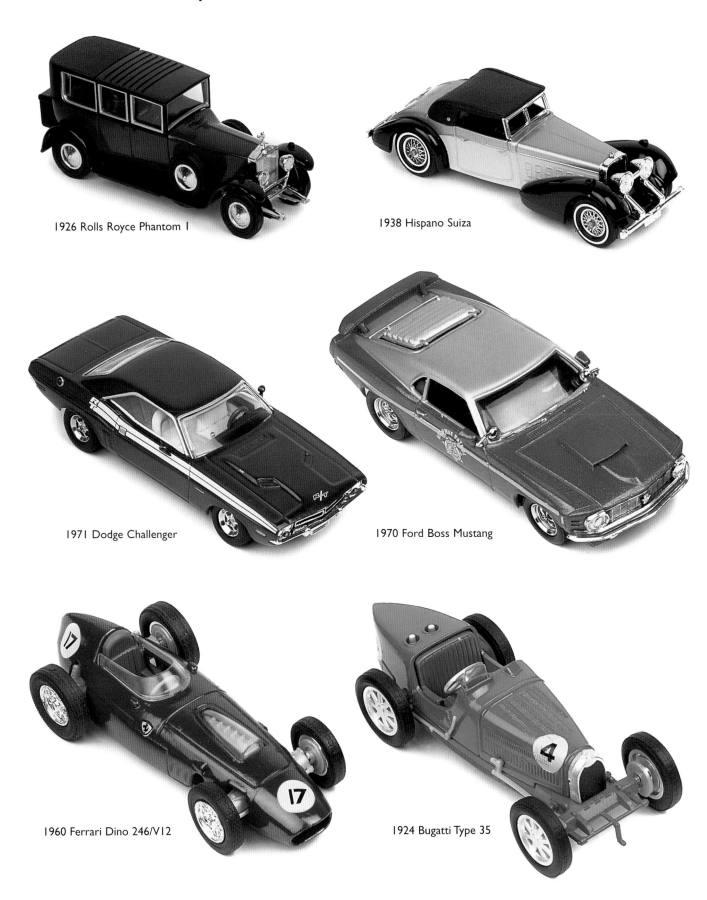

1926 Rolls Royce Phantom I

1938 Hispano Suiza

1971 Dodge Challenger

1970 Ford Boss Mustang

1960 Ferrari Dino 246/V12

1924 Bugatti Type 35

1931 "Grosser" Mercedes-Benz 770

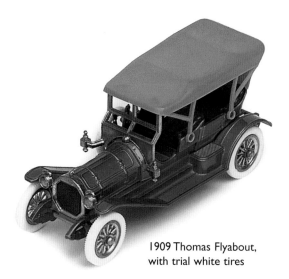
1909 Thomas Flyabout,
with trial white tires

1936 Auburn Speedster 851

1968 Camaro SS 396

1935 E.R.A.

1957 Maserati 250F

World-Class Matchbox Models

Racing Porsche, 1983

Jaguar XK120, 1984

1957 Chevrolet Belair, 1979

Jaguar XJ6, 1987

Mercedes-Benz 500SL, 1990

Corvette T-Top, 1982

Ferrari 308 GTB, 1981

1965 Corvette Grand Sport, 1990

Toyota Supra, 1995

Ferrari Testarosa, 1986

Nissan 300ZX, 1990

Nissan 300ZX, 1990

Lamborghini Diablo, 1992

BMW M-1, 1983

Ferrari F-40, 1989

Mustang Cobra, 1995

World-Class Matchbox Models

Thunderbird Turbo Coupe, 1987

Camaro Z-28, 1994

Mazda RX-7, 1994

Lamborghini Countach, 1985

Mustang Mach III, 1994

Corvette T-Top, 1982

Cadillac Allante, 1987

Porsche 959, 1986

Lincoln Town Car, 1989

Rolls Royce Silver Cloud, 1986

1984 Corvette, 1983

Porsche 944, 1989

Dodge Viper RT/IO, 1994

AMG Mercedes 500SEC, 1984

Aston Martin DB-78, 1994

Plymouth Prowler, 1995

MATCHBOX Trivia

Just over 200 of the legendary Coronation Coaches with two figures were made before Lesney learned that Queen Elizabeth II would ride alone. If you come across a coach with Prince Phillip and the Queen, grab it . . . it's no doubt worth a fortune!

MATCHBOX Q&A

Q: Which recently cancelled TV series starring John Goodman used Matchbox vehicles as set dressing and props?

A: "Normal, Ohio"

Connectables Set, 1989

149

12 The Corgi-Matchbox Connection

Long before it became a separate die-cast company, Corgi was a product line developed in 1956 by the Mettoy toy company. The Corgi name was inspired by the Welsh dog breed and can be explained by the fact that Mettoy had factories in Wales. Although Corgi was tempted to mimic Dinky models—as Matchbox had a few years earlier—the company decided to strike out in a new direction by giving all their vehicles windows. They touted their bold stroke with an advertising slogan: "The First with Windows."

Corgi quickly inaugurated a collectors club, newsletter, and catalog, and began advertising on TV in 1957. In 1959, the company's Renault Floride was not only equipped with windows, but seats, paneling, setting wheel, and spring suspension as well. These luxurious treatments soon found their way into all Corgi models.

Corgi went public in 1963 and, like Lesney before it, Corgi's stock was oversubscribed. In 1964, Mettoy celebrated its 30th anniversary with a range of vintage models called "Corgi Classics." And, in the following year, Corgi developed its most famous model ever, a tribute to secret agent James Bond. Corgi's replica of the 007 Aston Martin DB5 was a big hit and is highly collectible. Another Corgi coup was the famed "Chitty Chitty Bang Bang" model in 1968.

Like Lesney Products, Mettoy received its share of awards, including the Queens Award to Industry and the National Association of Toy Retailers' Highest Standards Award.

Mettoy Suffers Adversity and Sinks into Financial Ruin

Just as Lesney's progress was interrupted by a devastating fire, Mettoy suffered the same calamity. In 1969, the warehouse in Swansea, Wales, was gutted by fire. Because it took time to recover, retailers turned to competitors, including Dinky and Matchbox. At this time, Mettoy entered into an agreement with Fisher-Price—another company that would ultimately be acquired by Mattel—to produce toys to be sold in Europe.

The company managed to recover from diversity and competitive inroads, expanded its Swansea facility and experienced growth in the seventies. However, in the early eighties—about the same time that Lesney Products was bought by Universal—Mettoy suffered financial difficulties and went into receivership, just as Lesney had. While Lesney was purchased by Universal, the company that was named Corgi Toys Limited was formed after a management buyout. Just as Matchbox International succeeded Lesney, Corgi Toys became a separate entity after Mettoy's fall.

Corgi Seeks International Growth

Already ranked second among British die-cast companies, Corgi focused its attention on crafting high-quality models. To woo back retail customers, Corgi developed a new image. In the same year as the buyout, 1984, Chris Guest was made director of sales and marketing and the company began paying more attention to the desires of consumers, rather than focusing on product design and hoping people would buy.

Just as Lesney Products expanded globally after establishing itself in the U.K., Corgi looked to grow in foreign markets. The company boosted its exports and, like Lesney before, developed distribution arrangements in Australia and the U.S. Corgi's growth garnered the company a prestigious award in 1987. Corgi was named British Toy Company of the Year by the National Association of Toy Retailers.

Corgi Thrives under the Mattel Mantle

Two years later, in 1989, Mattel—which would eventually acquire the Matchbox brand from Tyco—bought Corgi. In 1991, the Swansea facilities in Wales were closed and Corgi operations moved to Mattel headquarters in Leicester, England. With Mattel's support, Corgi launched many new products and its range of die-cast models grew substantially in the early nineties.

Corgi launched the Original Omnibus range, which worked with 00 gauge train layouts, like so many Matchbox models. Mr. Bean's Mini, the Inspector Morse Jaguar and the Morris Minor from the TV series, *Some Mothers Do 'Ave 'Em* were all successes. And Corgi developed products specifically for the American market, including fire engines.

Corgi Goes Solo Again

On August 7, 1995—after just five years or so of ownership and just one year before Mattel would buy Tyco and the Matchbox brand—Mattel sold Corgi. Once again, the company was back in private hands, the result of a management buyout led by Chris Guest and fueled by venture capital. However, this change of entity would also be short-lived. In 1999, Corgi was acquired by Zindhart, a Chinese-based company that had been manufacturing a wide range of die-cast models for various companies. In turn, Corgi acquired Lledo (see Chapter 11). And, more recently, Corgi set up offices in the U.S. with the idea of dramatically expanding the company's presence in the States.

MATCHBOX Q&A

Q: In Matchbox coding, what does "LW" represent?
A: "Laser Wheels"

MATCHBOX Q&A

Q: Name one of the three models featured in the short-lived Matchbox Fashion Model Dolls series of the late eighties.
A: Christie Brinkley, Cheryl Tiegs, and Beverly Johnson

MATCHBOX Q&A

Q: In which Far East country were die-cast vehicles first produced bearing the Matchbox logo?
A: Hong Kong. They were the Disney characters produced by Universal for Lesney prior to the acquisition of Lesney Toys by Universal in 1982.

1922 Foden Steam Lorry and Trailer, Frasers

1930 Mack AC Truck,
Goodyear

1910 Renault Van, Perrier

1910 Renault Bus,
Vincent Fontaine,
with rare red roof

1910 Renault Van, Duckhams,
with rare closed handles

1922 Foden Steam Lorry, Pickfords

1929 Garrett Steam Lorry, Milkmaid Milk, with rare blue wheels

Mack AC Truck, Consolidated

1939 Albion Sixteen-Ton CX27 Lorry, Libby's

1980 Mack AC Tanker, Texaco, with very rare gold wheels

1932 Ford AA Truck, Peacock

1929 Morris Light Van, Lindt

1919 Walker Electric Van,
"His Master's Voice"

1933 Morris Courier Lorry,
Kemps

1939 Bedford Type KD Lorry,
G. Farrar

1930 Ford Model A Pickup,
W. Clifford

1933 Cadillac Fire Engine

1910 Renault Ambulance,
British Red Cross

1922 AEC Bus, Maples

1932 Mercedes-Benz L5
Lorry, Howaldtswerke

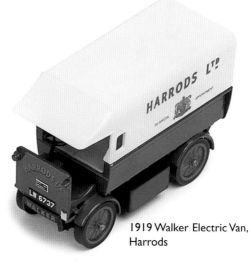

1919 Walker Electric Van,
Harrods

1918 Crossley Truck,
Lowenbrau

1917 Yorkshire Steam Lorry,
Samuel Smith of Tadcaster

Matchbox SuperFast Models

Utility Truck, 1989

Ambulance, 1977

GMC Wrecker, 1987

Dodge Dakota
Pickup, 1987

Crown Victoria
Police Car, 1997

Ford Mondeo,
1995

Chevy Lumina
Race Car, 1990

Sauber Group C
Racer, 1984

1933 Ford Street Rod,
1998

1962 Corvette,
1982

1921 Ford Model T Van, 1990

1921 Ford Model T Van, 1990

Ford F-350 Pickup, 2000

Land Rover Freelander, 1999

Mercedes-Benz 500SL Convertible, 1990

Mazda RX7, 1994

Plymouth Prowler, 1995

Mustang Cobra
Convertible, 1995

Corvette
Grand Sport, 1990

Corvette
Grand Sport, 1990

Matchbox SuperFast Models

Dodge
Delivery Truck, 1982

Ford Model A Van,
biggest seller, 1982

Isuzu Rodeo, 1995

Chevy Suburban, 1999

Mitsubishi Spyder, 1995

Ford Thunderbird
Racecar, 1994

Camaro Z-28,
1994

Lamborghini Diablo, 1992

Jaguar XJ6
Police Car, 1991

Jaguar XJ6
Police Car, 1991

Volkswagen Dormobile
Ambulance, 1970

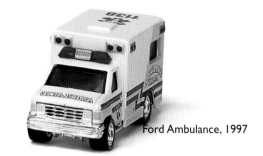

Ford Ambulance, 1997

Jeep Grand Cherokee,
1999

Ford 4x4 F-150
Pickup, 1995

Audi Avus Quattro, 1995

Corvette III,
Sting Ray, 1994

Ferrari 456GT, 1994

Ferrari F-50, 1996

1969 Chevy Camaro
SS396, 1997

1970 Ford Mustang Boss
302, 1998

Special Limited-Edition Yesteryears

1952 Land Rover and Trailer,
Surf Patrol

1922 Scania Vabis Half-Track
Post Bus, Holiday Special

1930 Deusenberg Model J
Town Car

1937 GMC Army Field Ambulance

1920 Leyland Three-Ton Lorry,
Luff & Sons

1920 Mack AC Lorry, Fishermans Wharf

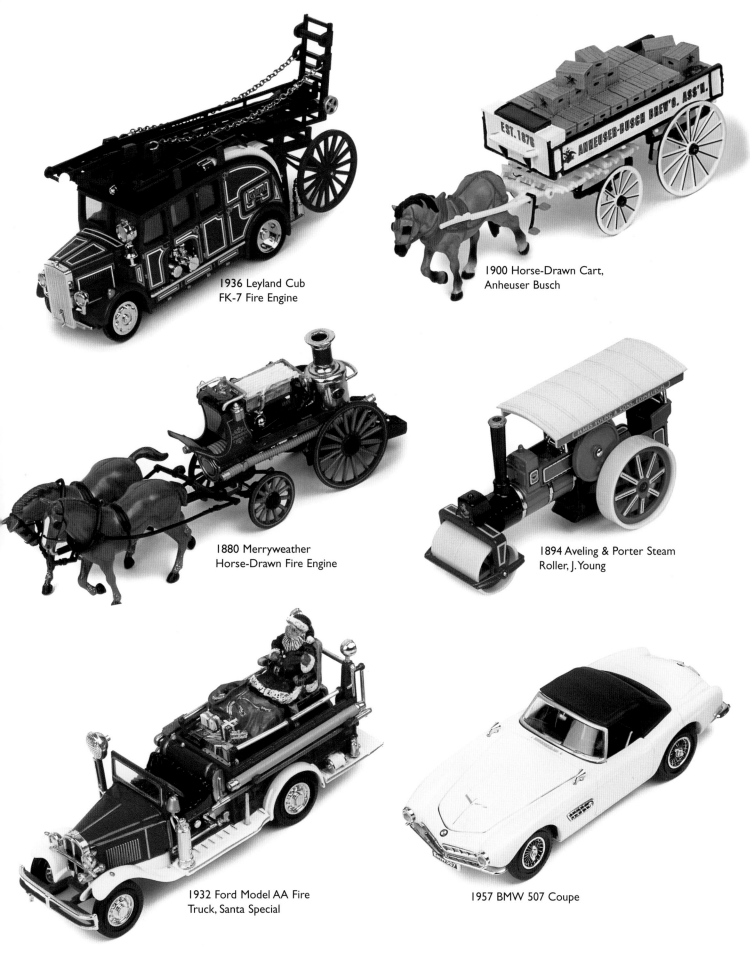

1936 Leyland Cub
FK-7 Fire Engine

1900 Horse-Drawn Cart,
Anheuser Busch

1880 Merryweather
Horse-Drawn Fire Engine

1894 Aveling & Porter Steam
Roller, J. Young

1932 Ford Model AA Fire
Truck, Santa Special

1957 BMW 507 Coupe

1952 Land Rover and Trailer, Surf Patrol:
Arguably the most-detailed Model of Yesteryear,
even a pair of binoculars are included in the dinghy.

1936 Leyland Cub FK-7 Fire Engine: This model
features the most finely detailed "working"
component—the huge escape ladder is
fully extendable and has rotating wheels.

Special Limited-Edition Models of Yesteryear Vehicles

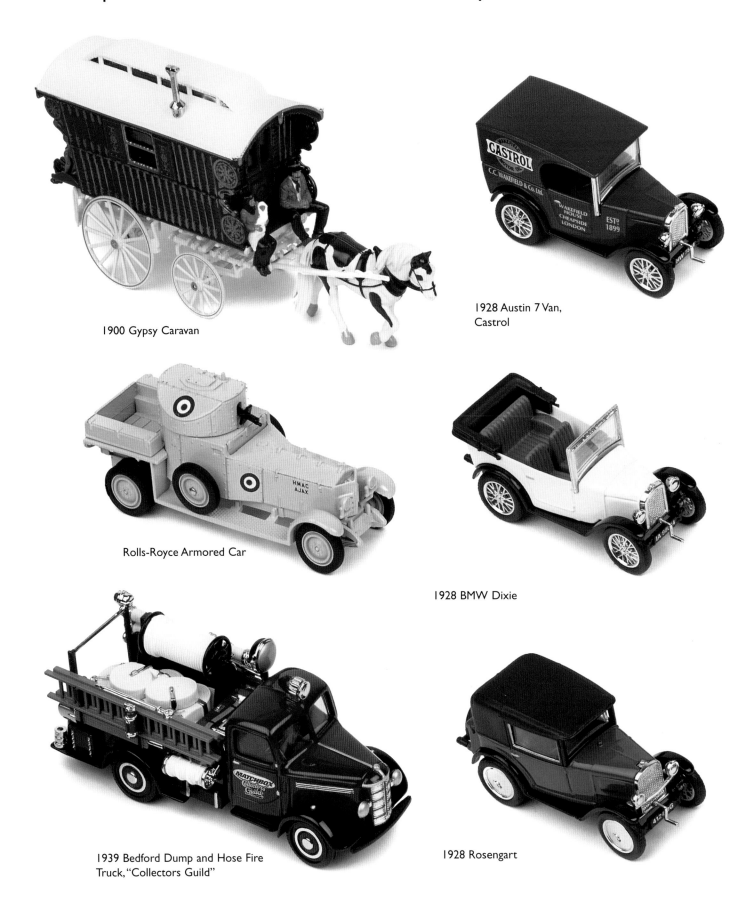

1900 Gypsy Caravan

1928 Austin 7 Van,
Castrol

Rolls-Royce Armored Car

1928 BMW Dixie

1939 Bedford Dump and Hose Fire
Truck, "Collectors Guild"

1928 Rosengart

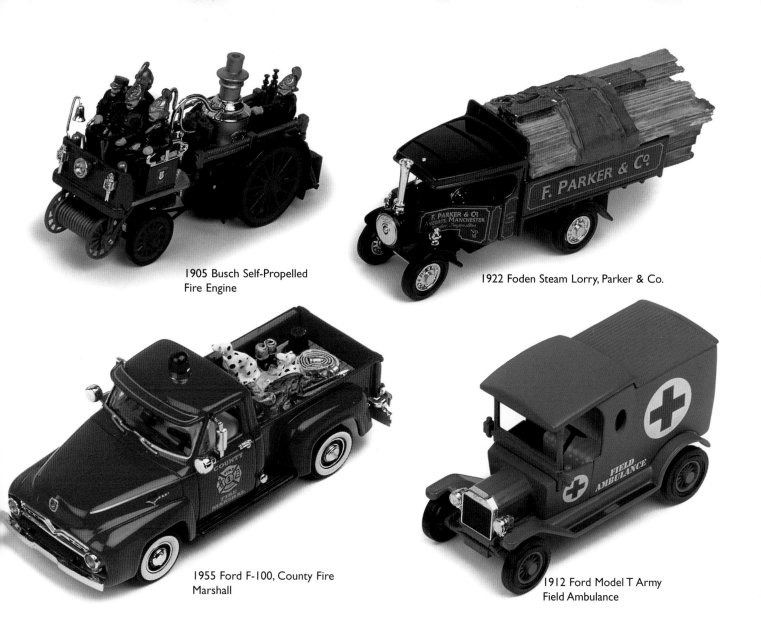

1905 Busch Self-Propelled
Fire Engine

1922 Foden Steam Lorry, Parker & Co.

1955 Ford F-100, County Fire
Marshall

1912 Ford Model T Army
Field Ambulance

1762 Gold State Coach

Models of Yesteryear Vehicles in Detail

1894 Aveling & Porter Steam Roller: A modern-day Model of Yesteryear "classic" whereby an estimated seventy-two P. B. Coulson & Sons were mistakenly finished in green and black, instead of royal blue.

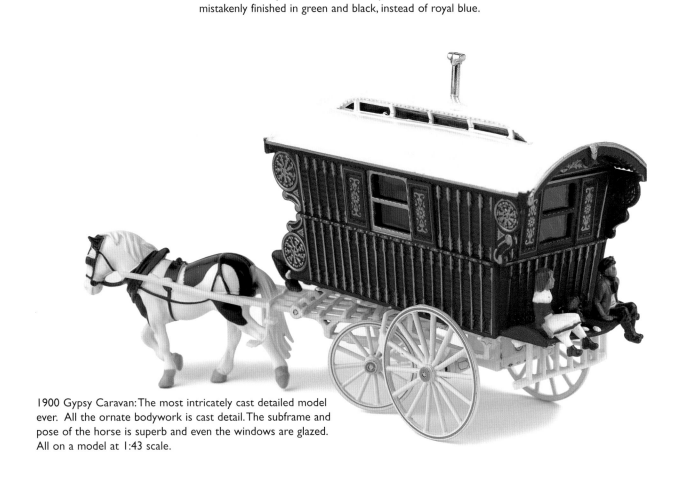

1900 Gypsy Caravan: The most intricately cast detailed model ever. All the ornate bodywork is cast detail. The subframe and pose of the horse is superb and even the windows are glazed. All on a model at 1:43 scale.

1905 Busch Self-Propelled Fire Engine: Probably the most unusual fire engine in the range including (unusually) the crew members. This particular example has the boiler collar and associated pipes finished in copper rather than the regular brass finish.

1932 Ford Model AA Fire Engine: the first Model of Yesteryear to include a figure of Santa Claus

13 Tyco Acquires Matchbox and Establishes an International Network

During the eighties, perhaps in part due to Hot Wheels' growing market share in the U.S., Universal focused more and more attention on its European markets. The U.S. operation created its own designs for the American market while the U.K. operation developed products for European and other markets. At this time, sales in the U.K. and Germany dwarfed sales in the United States.

Laser Wheels Still Seems Like a Missed Opportunity

While the acquisition of Dinky looked like a great coup in 1987, Universal never really exploited the brand's potential, even in Europe where Dinky was best known. Still another mystery took root that same year. In Europe and Australia, Universal introduced "Laser Wheels," which appeared to be faster down the track than any other models. Laser Wheels looked like the perfect solution to a vexing problem: how to reclaim dominance in the U. S. market.

Meanwhile, as Universal failed to take advantage of the opportunities made possible by the purchase of Dinky and the creation of Laser Wheels, sales of Models of Yesteryear vehicles continued to decline. The company's mistakes began to outnumber its triumphs. On the one hand, Matchbox hit a home run with its Pee Wee Herman line in the U.S. market. But then the company created a Freddy Kreuger talking doll, based on the character in the infamous horror movies. Pressure from concerned parents, religious, and other groups resulted in Matchbox having to remove the dubious product from stores.

By the early nineties, Matchbox's performance continued to be disappointing. Many observers cite the company's foray into too many toy categories and an overall lack of focus and direction. In any case, David Yeh began shopping the company around. Ultimately he found a buyer with a strategic interest.

Tyco Toys was looking to expand in Europe and elsewhere around the world. With Matchbox's strong international distribution, it seemed like a good match. On October 2, 1992, it was official: Tyco acquired Universal Group and now owned Matchbox Toys.

A Brief Glimpse into Tyco History

Founded in 1926 by John Tyler, the Tyler Company came to be known as Tyco. In the early years, the company progressed from making components for toy trains to manufacturing toy train kits. By the sixties, Tyco was making HO scale trains and, over the next two decades, would also move into truck and racing sets. Tyco was acquired by the Sara Lee Corporation and then sold to Savoy Industries. After the Savoy acquisition, Tyco began to dramatically expand its product line, venturing into such new categories as Super Block Sets, personality telephones, and radio-control vehicles, which became a very big business for Tyco.

Other successful product innovations included "Dino-Riders," action figures that were introduced in 1987 to take advantage of the popularity of dinosaurs. Tyco purchased View-Master/ Ideal Group, Inc. in 1989 and generated significant sales volumes from products like the View-Master® Viewer (used to view reels of photos), Magna Doodle® (featuring a magnetic pencil for writing and drawing), and the Ideal Nursery line of dolls. In the early nineties, Tyco acquired Illco, which had a successful line of preschool toys. Once named Tyco Preschool it is now known as Fisher-Price Character Brands. And, of course, in 1992, Tyco bought the Universal Matchbox Group.

Tyco Struggles with Transition but Emerges with Renewed Vigor

"Tyco bought Matchbox because Hot Wheels doesn't travel well around the world and Matchbox does," says Alex Welch, the senior vice president in charge of Asia and the Pacific for Mattel, who was hired as senior vice president in charge of international for Tyco. Tyco was looking for a global die-cast brand. "We were also convinced that we could make the Matchbox brand grow in the U. S.," says Welch, "because that's a market where we already had plenty of success and experience."

While some insiders say that Tyco also wanted the Matchbox international distribution network and abandoned it shortly after the acquisition, Welch has a different point of view. "Matchbox had big, inefficient facilities," he says, "so we decided to acquire our own subsidiaries." The company already had a German operation that was highly effective. For the Australian market, Tyco bought Croner Tyco, "which was a $75 million business," says Welch. This company had the Hunter toy line and represented prestigious brands from around the world, including Casio, the watch company, which also made toys.

There is one thing the people who were at Tyco seem to agree on: global expansion came with many headaches. "We decided to buy our old distributors," says Welch. "We set up business in France, but that didn't work. Italy was a total disaster. But we had success in the Netherlands, Belgium, and Luxemburg."

Tyco also experienced diversity in the United Kingdom, the original home of Matchbox. "They used Toys 'R Us warehouses and didn't control inventory very well," says Alex Welch. But there were other problems as well. Tyco had been using a company called Action GT as a distributor. Its president was Brian Triptree, and his partner, the CFO of the firm, went to jail for fraud. It was obvious that the company would collapse.

At this time, Karsten Malmos, president of Tyco International, assumed control and formed Tyco-Matchbox U. K., with Triptree as head.

After the acquisition of Matchbox, Tyco also abandoned product lines that some insiders say they should have kept. These included the Tyco® Preschool line, which grew to become the dominant U.K. brand in its category, as well as the "Connectables" line. The profitable Tyco Preschool line included track sets with cars, trains, and other vehicles, street lights and signs, people and animals, storefronts, and more. The Connectables were multicomponent models that could be taken apart and put back together, often with components from other models. Some were very elaborate, consisting of many vehicles of varying size, as well as other accessories.

However, according to Alex Welch, "Preschool and some of the other lines didn't amount to much. We had signed a deal with Children's Television Workshop (CTW) for the license to create Sesame Street toys. We created a full line of products, knowing it would be a good business for us." Tyco Preschool would become the most dominant force in Sesame Street preschool toys.

In any case, by the end of 1993, Tyco was in trouble. Sales of "Crash Dummies," which had been a big hit, were in decline. Nintendo and Sega electronic games were commanding children's attention, and sales of Tyco Radio Control (R/C) suffered as a result. What's more, a fledgling collectibles business was producing very disappointing results and losing money.

Undaunted, Tyco would soon engineer a turn-around, beginning with making the collectibles enterprise highly profitable.

A Funny Thing Happened to the General Manager of Tyco U.K.

Another intriguing chapter in Matchbox history unfolded after the Tyco acquisition. Nick Austin, who was the general manager in the U. K., went to Richard Grey, Tyco's chairman, and made a power move. He said he wanted to head up all international business. The problem was that the job was already taken by Karsten Malmos. So Tyco bought him out.

Prior to this development, Matchbox had developed a playset in the U. K. based on the highly popular "Thunderbirds" TV Supermarionation show. The playset portrayed Tracy Island, home to the various characters from the ITV show. It consisted of characters and their vehicles, including Penelope and her Rolls-Royce, as well as rocket ships. This product was very successful, with sales of about $70 million, and a sequel, called Captain Scarlet, was in development when Nick Austin was leaving the company. Tyco gave Austin rights to develop the product, which he did after forming his own company called Vivid Imagination. Captain Scarlet gave the ex-Tyco executive the product he needed to build a business. It generated sales of roughly $12 million in its first year.

The Thunderbirds Commemorative Set,: BBC Radio Times Limited Edition, issued in 1992, includes: Thunderbird I, Thunderbird II, Thunderbird III, Thunderbird IV, FAB 1 Car, and POD

Successful miniature line of the Matchbox preschool line using normal models with preschool colors

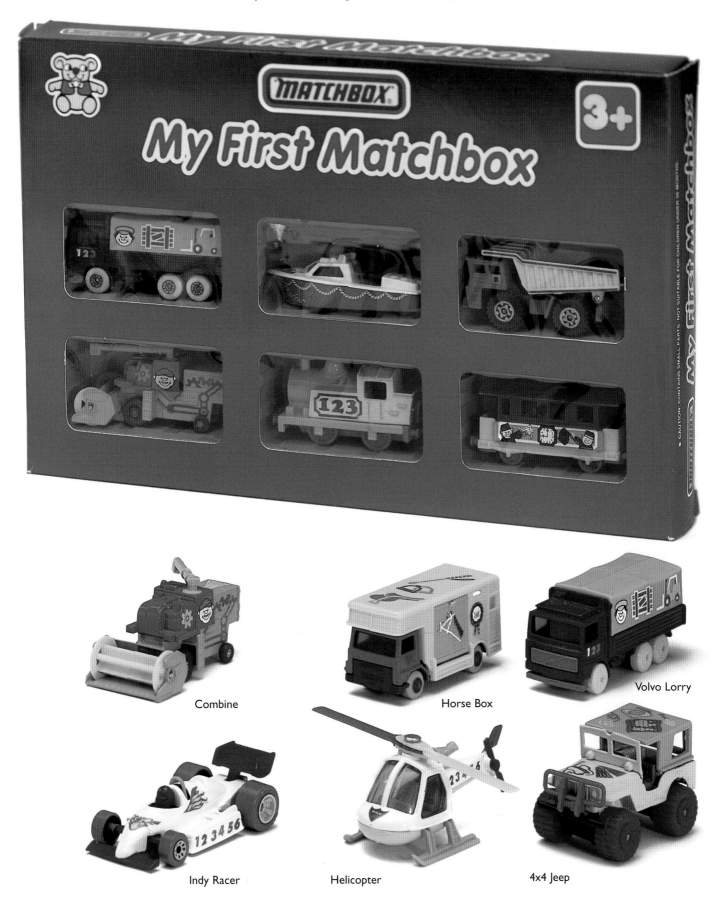

Combine

Horse Box

Volvo Lorry

Indy Racer

Helicopter

4x4 Jeep

My First Matchbox Models

040 Loco and Passenger Coach

London Bus

Ford Bronco II

Peterbilt Tanker

Model A Ford

Rover Sterling

Rover Sterling

Faun Dumptruck

Cement Mixer

Bulldozer

Ford Flairside Pickup

School Bus

LTD Police Car

174

Tractor Shovel

Fire Engine

Skip Truck

Peugot Quasar

Ferrari Testarosa

Lincoln Town Car

Chevy Breakdown Truck

Utility Truck

Police Launch

London Taxi

MATCHBOX Q&A

Q: Why were workers locked in cages to make the Models of Yesteryear "blue" Hoover model? (see page 196)

A: To produce the limited 560 models that now fetch over US$1,000

14

Tyco Launches Matchbox Collectibles and Creates a Winner for the Nineties

Just before the Tyco acquisition of Matchbox, the U.S. division of Matchbox tried unsuccessfully to launch a direct marketing business. Undaunted by this initial failure, Robert Hill of Matchbox Australia felt that there was considerable potential in direct-marketing of die-cast collectibles vehicles. After all, companies like The Franklin Mint and Danbury Mint had achieved considerable success with mail-order businesses. Hill convinced Frank Tregallas, general manager in Australia, to develop a direct-marketing enterprise.

Tregallas agreed with Hill and their roles were quickly defined. Tregallas would provide the vision for the collectibles business and Robert Hill would handle execution. Using small ads that simply asked people to call for information, the company sold products through thirty-five collector call centers. They quickly built a file of 50,000 customers.

When Tyco came into the picture, Tregallas negotiated with Tyco CFO Harry Pearce to maintain control over the budding collectibles business. However, Tyco was in Mt. Laurel, New Jersey, and Tregallas was in Sydney, Australia. To gain some control over the business, Tyco set up a warehouse and other operations in Portland, Oregon. And Tyco had warehousing in the U.K. as well, managed by Andrew Tallis.

However, Tregallas promised sales of $11 million in 1993. Instead, he only reached "about $6 million with a $3 million loss," says Mike Dukes, the ex–Franklin Mint manager who would soon take over the business. This lackluster performance would prove to be Tregallas' undoing. Before he left the company, however, he planted the seeds that would soon flourish.

The Key Was to Offer Collections Rather than Solo Products

Tregallas ended up with a big hit and a big flop. The hit was "Beers of the World," which he tried to market as individual models. Once Mike Dukes got hold of the program, it became a series of six die-cast models decorated with the liveries of world-renowned brewmasters, including Castlemaine XXXX from Australia and Beck's from Germany, Fuller's from England, and Carlsberg from Denmark. The series worked so well that it would ultimately quadruple in size—to twenty-four models—before running out of steam.

The Tregallas flop was "Taste of France," a series of six models that were virtually identical,

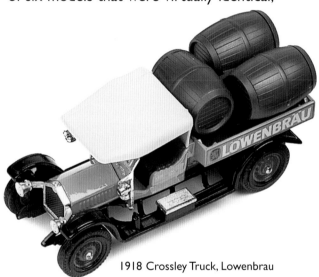

1918 Crossley Truck, Lowenbrau

except for minor tooling modifications to a basic Citröen. Naturally, each model bore different graphics representing such prominent French companies as Martell Cognac, Evian Mineral Water, Marcillat Brie, and Yoplait Yogurt.

Tregallas' other failures included a Dodge Route Van that was the first model tooled by the direct marketing group. Tregallas commissioned a firm in Asia to create the design, which was considered poor by the Matchbox in-house design team. In addition, Tregallas utilized existing Matchbox tooling for three limited editions—a Gypsy Caravan, Wells Fargo

Stagecoach, and London (horse-drawn) Omnibus—none of which was successful.

Despite this spotty performance, Tregallas had proven that with the right concept—such as "Beers of the World"—consumers would buy Matchbox collectible vehicles through the mail. After Tyco acquired Matchbox, the new management slowly but surely concurred that Matchbox® Collectibles would enable the company to broaden the appeal of the Matchbox brand in high-value markets in the U.S. and Europe. Tregellas and Hill had initiated what would soon become a global enterprise.

Incidentally, one benefit of the explosive growth that Matchbox Collectibles would soon enjoy was the revival of two important die-cast brands that seemed to be on the verge of extinction: Models of Yesteryear and Dinky. The new direct channel would utilize these brands very effectively in creating models that were far superior to anything Matchbox had ever produced before.

Tyco Hires a Seasoned Pro and Matchbox Collectibles Enjoys Unprecedented Success

The early foray into direct marketing didn't produce any profits for Tyco, but losses were relatively modest. Senior Vice President Alex Welch knew that with the right team in place, Tyco would have an excellent chance of building a powerful business that would depend principally on individual collectors for success, rather than mass retailers who often used their clout to apply considerable downward pressure on the prices Tyco could charge them. Welch was anxious to see where direct marketing of high-end die-cast collectibles might take them. But he knew he needed someone who really understood the direct channel and collector mentality.

Wisely, Welch turned to the collectibles company that had enjoyed tremendous growth in the eighties, largely because of its success in direct marketing of very high-end die-cast. That company is The Franklin Mint. And the savvy direct marketer hired away from The Franklin Mint was Mike Dukes, whom Tyco named director of marketing. Dukes would soon develop a strategy and product concepts that would perform as no other die-cast company ever had before.

"As soon as Dukes joined us, he began finding numerous ways to save money," says Welch, "and you could just feel the chemistry among the players we put together, including Sid Sullivan in R&D and Simon Iredale, who was in charge of purchasing." Sullivan—who headed up the U.K. design team and developed Matchbox product ideas for nearly thirty years—secured licenses from prominent companies, whose graphics would appear on models and collections. "Sid was making prototypes, and Simon and Mike were working out the costs, figuring out how to make the business work."

There was just one problem. "Our chairman, Dick Grey, wanted collectibles to go away," says Welch. "But Dukes had already started promoting programs. One day, at a meeting, Dick asked Mike what kind of margin he was getting. When Mike said sixty-four percent, a number unheard of in the toy business, Dick was suddenly interested. But he was still skeptical. I remember him asking Dukes point-blank if he could make the business profitable. 'Dick, it's in the bag,' Dukes said. That was a major turning point."

Mike Dukes began by identifying seven ideas he wanted to promote, including individual models like the 1930 Ahrens-Fox Fire Engine and "Power of the Press," a series that would honor six of the world's most prominent newspapers. This particular series was Alex Welch's idea; his wife worked for the *New York Times* so he had a special interest in journalism. However, when Dukes presented his ideas to Tyco management—who were schooled in retail sales of toys—they didn't understand why consumers would find Dukes' concepts appealing.

1948 Dodge Route Van, New York Times

So, Dukes turned to a couple of creative consultants from Nick Mitchell & Associates whom he knew from his Franklin Mint days. "We made a presentation to Tyco management, outlining key differences between mass retail toy marketing directed at consumers and targeted direct marketing of collectibles designed to appeal to the collector mentality," says Mitchell, who had worked for The Franklin Mint for twenty years. The consultants also prepared advertising layouts, showing how they would recommend promoting the various product concepts Dukes had developed.

Fortunately, this presentation convinced Tyco management to give Mike Dukes the green light to test most of the programs he had in mind, which included a replica of the famous train, The Crescent Limited, and a six-model collection of Corvettes. Dukes commissioned Nick Mitchell & Associates to develop the ads and direct mail packages to support the programs he had in mind. Fortunately for all, every program succeeded, and Matchbox Collectibles continued to achieve close to a 100 percent success rate for the next several years.

What Were the Key Ingredients to Matchbox Collectibles Meteoric Rise?

Mike Dukes began by exploring the vast reservoir of die-cast tooling that Matchbox had developed over the years. He knew that if he kept his tooling costs to a minimum, Matchbox

Collectibles could afford to keep its prices well under the competition—very much like Lesney Products had, especially in the early years when they undercut Corgi and others.

Entirely new tooling for a single new model can easily cost $100,000, the kind of expense Matchbox Collectibles would take on as it progressed. But, in the beginning, Dukes worked closely with the design team headed up by Bill Kerner, which designed models for the entire Matchbox business, mass retail and direct collectibles. Together, Dukes and Kerner's team figured out how how to use existing tooling, yet still manage to give the new concepts collectible flavor. They found ways to offer entire collections for less than what other die-cast collectibles companies were charging for a single model.

Although Dukes was offering die-cast at exceptional prices, he was always careful to maintain the fundamental tenets of collectibility. He did so by appealing to the collector's desires in several ways. One way was to create a collection based on a theme collectors would find appealing, just as he had done with "Beers of the World." Each model in a collection was decorated with graphics to support the theme.

For example, "The Official International Postal Trucks Collection" consisted of six models decorated with graphics from post offices all over the world. The entire series was priced at just $24.50. Again, the reason for the low price was that Matchbox used existing tooling; in fact, all six models were identical except for the graphics. Of course, Matchbox Collectibles wouldn't be able to continue this strategy for very long because collectors would no doubt grow tired of it. But, in the beginning, it enabled Matchbox Collectibles to attract a large following of collectors.

"Two other programs that really set the stage for Matchbox Collectibles were 'The Power of the Press', and 'The Golden Age of Steam,'" says Mike Dukes. "The former introduced the

Dodge Route Van, which was conceived by the Australian management, but they intended to introduce a collection of six one-shots of the Dodge with different American brand names on each model. We knew only a series would make financial sense, and we recognized that we needed to offer diversity in the models. Then it became a challenge to decide on the best possible theme that would appeal to collectors. The Dodge Route Van looks like a bread or newspaper truck. Moreover, the collection had to maintain global interest. Given these parameters, 'The Power of the Press' made sense. While this series wasn't successful, it set the strategy for future die-cast collections."

"The Golden Age of Steam" was a Matchbox milestone in another sense. This was a "great example of taking existing tools, making slight modifications, and introducing a new collection," Dukes says. "The steam collection demonstrated the diversity of the Matchbox tooling bank. This program was a resounding success globally and a spectacular success in the U.K. One dramatic change we made was to add rubber tires and upgraded wheels to these steam vehicles."

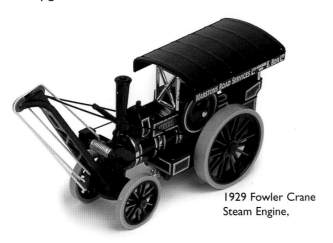

1929 Fowler Crane
Steam Engine,

Another thing Dukes and the design team did was to enhance existing tooling with new tools to make each model more detailed, such as "The International Fire Engine Collection." The most successful series Matchbox Collectibles would ever produce, it ultimately became a thirty-six-model collection. Dukes and the designers used existing tooling from the Matchbox archives. Senior designer Berdj Mazmanian cre-

ated additional details, such as hoses, ladders, fire extinguishers, and intricate fittings. "Instead of spending $400,000 or more on new tooling, I was able to invest about $40,000," says Dukes. And yet he and Mazmanian were able to elevate the quality of Matchbox Collectibles die-cast to a level close to that of major competitors like The Franklin Mint and Danbury Mint, whose products were still far higher in price.

Dukes and the design team—including experienced die-cast designers like Vince D'Angelo—pioneered innovations that enhanced collectibility while also advancing the art of die-cast. These nuances included simple techniques like crafting wheels that featured one or two colors and a chrome finish. One of the most successful series in this vein was "The Fabulous Fifties Road Service Collection."

Only two new tools were used for the six different designs. Each had a different grille and distinctive graphics honoring famous names in automotive service, including AAA, Mobil and Sinclair. The designers replicated equipment and supplies to go into the truck beds, including a utility cabinet and vise, a battery charger on wheels, and a full rack of batteries. The series was a huge success.

Chemistry, collaboration and teamwork are often the keys to success. This was certainly true for Matchbox Collectibles. Once the business gained traction, the marketers would meet frequently with the designers to brainstorm series themes and individual product ideas. "These meetings would go on for hours," Berdj Mazmanian says. "But every minute was time well spent."

Matchbox Collectibles Pioneers New Techniques

Perhaps the most dramatic innovation pioneered at Matchbox Collectibles was the clever combination of hand-painted cold-cast sculptures with die-cast models. The first Matchbox Collectibles individual model crafted of both

179

metal and sculpture was the Scania-Vabis Postbus Special, which became a collecting phenomenon unto itself.

A Christmas edition offered through the 1996 holiday catalog, this model was an intricate die-cast replica of a 1922 Postbus Special with the hand-painted resin sculpture of a Christmas tree on the roof. It was a limited edition of 5,000. Roughly half the trees were crafted in the United Kingdom and, due to production difficulties, the other half were made in the Far East. The latter simply took one of the trees already made in the U.K. and created a mold to make their trees. Models bearing the slightly smaller tree soon commanded hundreds of dollars on the secondary market. And yet, the Scania-Vabis Holiday Special was sold for just $29.50, many times less than most competitors' offerings.

1922 Scania Vabis Half-Track Postbus, Holiday Special

Matchbox Collectibles went on to create a number of other replicas combining the mixed media of die-cast and cold-cast, including three models in "The Steam Powered Vehicles Collection," the Matchbox Holiday Fire Engine and the Christmas 1955 Chevy 3100 Pickup from the 1996 holiday catalog.

Another ingredient that Mike Dukes added to Matchbox Collectibles' highly successful formula was *The Matchbox Collector*, a full-color newsletter containing articles about various aspects of collecting. The idea behind the newsletter was to offer individual models to collectors without making separate mailings. With Matchbox Collectibles' relatively low prices, individual mailings promoting solo products couldn't make money. So, along with each issue of the newsletter, collectors also received a brochure promoting several models.

In the early years of the newsletter, the collectibles offered were invariably limited editions. When the first newsletter and insert appeared in 1997, the response was so overwhelming that Matchbox Collectibles had to write letters to many collectors who wouldn't be getting the models they ordered because they sold out very quickly.

Matchbox Collectibles Quickly Discovers the Best-Selling Themes

The first complete Matchbox Collectibles series to be crafted with entirely new die-cast tooling was its muscle car collection, which was another big success. Even with the high tooling cost, Matchbox Collectibles was able to charge $29.95 each, still well under the competition. Matchbox Collectibles seemed to be hitting all the collectors' hot buttons.

The first Matchbox Collectibles die-cast tractor trailer, commemorating the 200th anniversary of Jim Beam, sold 100,000 models. "This was a major milestone for us," says Mike Dukes. "It demonstrated that our brand had significant power and could drive substantial volume." Matchbox Collectibles went on to issue individual models and series honoring brewmasters like Budweiser and distillers like Beefeater and J&B.

These large-scale rigs would lead to the development of highly successful series at the smaller 1:100 scale. For example, the "North American Brewmasters Collection" and Harley-Davidson "Milestones of Motorcyling" collections were big hits.

Both the larger 1:58 scale and smaller 1:100 scale rigs have been lauded by Matchbox aficionados including Everett Marshall, who is one of the world's most knowledgeable and respected Matchbox experts. Marshall, who owns the Matchbox Road Museum in Newfield, New Jersey—which houses one of the world's largest collections of Matchbox models—considers the Miller Brewing tractor trailer in the Brewmasters collection one of the best models he owns. He's also particularly fond of the first Jack Daniel's rig developed by Matchbox Collectibles.

During this period, Matchbox Collectibles created a series that commemorated the 40th anniversary of the Models of Yesteryear series, with each model chosen by Lesney co-founder Leslie Smith. Matchbox Collectibles also developed collectibles to help support worthy causes, including Ronald McDonald Australia Children's Charities. When prestigious brands were combined with the universally recognized Matchbox brand, success usually followed.

1948 Diamond T, Jack Daniel's

MATCHBOX® Q&A

Q: Approximately how many die-cast vehicles will Matchbox have produced by the start of 2002, the 50th year of miniatures?

A: Three billion

The Matchbox Collectible Years

1939 Bedford Crash Tender,
Bristol Aeroplane Co.

1936 Leyland Cub
Open Cab Fire Engine

1947 Citröen Type "H" Van, Yoplait

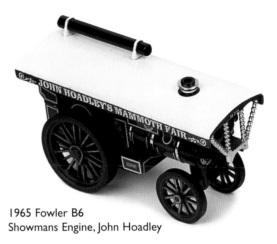

1965 Fowler B6
Showmans Engine, John Hoadley

1946 Dodge 4x4 Power Wagon

1932 Diamond "T" Truck, Budweiser

1931 Diddler Trolley Bus, London United

1932 Mercedes-Benz L5 Lorry,
Holstenbier

1954 Ford F-100 Pickup,
Pennsylvania Railroad

1932 Mercedes-Benz Ladder Fire Truck

1937 GMC Van, Laphroaig

1932 Ford Model AA Truck, Coca-Cola

The Matchbox Collectible Years

1948 GMC CoE, Jim Beam

1918 Atkinson Steam Lorry, Swan Brewery

1953 Ford F-100 Fire Truck, Garden City

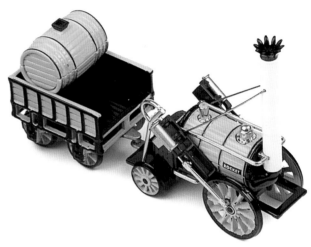

1829 Stevenson's Rocket Locomotive

1920 Mack "AC" Fire Truck

1930 Ford Model A Fire Truck, Battalion Chief

1926 Ford Model TT Van,
Anchor Steam

1929 Fowler Crane Steam Engine,
Marstons

1935 Mack "AB" Fire Engine

1948 Dodge Route Van, New York Times

1907 Seagrave AC53 Fire Engine

1955 Chevrolet 3100,
AAA Towing Service

Matchbox Collectibles

1937 International DR60 Stake Truck,
Harley-Davidson

1937 Dodge Airflow Tanker, Texaco

1934 International Harvester
"C" Series Pickup, Jack Daniels

1932 Ford Model AA Fire Truck

1940 Ford Pickup Truck, Murdock Lumber

1961 International Scout 4x4 U.S. Mail

1969 Chevy K/5 4x4 Blazer

1931 Scammel Lorry, GWR

1920 Mack "AC" Tanker,
The Texas Company

1966 Ford Bronco 4x4

1950 Ford E83W,
British Red Cross Ambulance

1933 Diamond "T" Truck, Caterpillar

Matchbox Collectibles

1959 Mercedes-Benz L408 Ambulance

1956 Holden FJ/2104 Panel Van

1948 GMC CoE Bottle Truck, Coca-Cola

1951 Holden FX Utility, Mr. Fix-It

1955 Chevrolet 3100 Service Truck, Texaco

1955 Chevrolet 3100 Wrecker Truck,
Matchbox Collectibles

1937 Dodge Airflow Truck,
Coca-Cola

1945 Jeep CJ2A, 4x4

1912 Ford Model T Van,
U.S. Mail

1941 Chevrolet Pickup,
Harley-Davidson

1946 Dodge Power Wagon 4x4,
White Tail Reserve

1957 Chevrolet 3100
Pickup Truck

15 A Rejuvenated Tyco is Acquired by Mattel

In the first year of Mike Dukes' involvement, 1994, Matchbox Collectibles generated $12 million in sales with a twenty percent profit. By 1997, the year of Dukes' departure, the division was up to roughly $45 million in sales. This was also the year that Mattel acquired Tyco, bringing two former competitors—Matchbox and Hot Wheels—together at last.

By this time, Tyco was very strong and profitable, having shaken off its early nineties growing pains. "We had better systems in place," says Alex Welch. "Sesame Street products were performing well, as was Matchbox. Many markets were producing exceptional results, including Australia, where Matchbox outsold Hot Wheels 3-to-1 at double the price. We also had a great premiums business."

The premiums business involved putting company graphics on die-cast models and selling them in bulk to the company, which would then use them as giveaways, incentives in promotions, and for other purposes. "Other money makers included View-Master and Doodle Bear® plush . . . you could write on it and then clean it in a washing machine," says Welch. "Even radio-control toys came back strong."

The Mattel acquisition of Tyco was good for Matchbox Collectibles. "All of the sudden we had licenses we never had before," says Mike Dukes. "Mattel spent the money to get us the big names like Harley-Davidson. And we had already proven that use of prestigious brands—combined with the Matchbox brand—could be highly successful."

Not long after the Mattel acquisition of Tyco, however, Dukes was lured back to The Franklin Mint. By the time he departed, his boss was Mel

Schlicker, a vice president and former executive for Bradford Exchange, America's largest collectibles company. Schlicker had a significant influence on continually improving the level of detailing, intricacy, and authenticity of Matchbox Collectibles models. For example, the fourth series of The International Fire Engine Collection, subtitled "The Turn-of-the-Century Edition," represented perhaps the finest models ever made by Matchbox Collectibles.

Mel Schlicker had a major impact on Matchbox Collectibles for another reason as well: he hired Ned Barrett, whom he knew at Bradford, to manage the Matchbox Collectibles business, which Barrett did successfully until 1999.

Barrett Builds a Profitable Specialty Retail Business

Although Matchbox Collectibles never exceeded the sales generated under Dukes, Ned Barrett worked with a colleague, Steve Spatz, to develop another channel that worked very well. First, let's look at a little historical background.

In the U.K., die-cast companies like Corgi had tapped the lucrative specialty retail business, selling their collectibles through small shops. While this channel is better established in the U.K. and can't be precisely duplicated in the U.S., Barrett and Spatz built a business by selling through gift and hobby shops and a variety of other locations, such as truck stops, where the big rigs sold well.

Like Lledo and other die-cast companies before it, Matchbox Collectibles was able to craft models and collections that could be sold both directly through the mail and in specialty retail outlets. And, under Ned Barrett's direction (1997–1999), the Collectibles division continued to prosper. Barrett was responsible for initiating Coca-Cola–sponsored collections. He also worked with the design team to develop existing licenses—including Jack Daniel's and Harley-Davidson—and produced highly profitable models and series. Recognizing an emerging collector interest in tanks, Barrett spearheaded a successful series of American, British, Russian, and German tanks from World War II.

Die-Cast Collectibles Industry Shifts into Low Gear

At about the time Ned Barrett left Matchbox Collectibles to form his own direct-marketing software and consulting company, Matchbox Collectibles began to spiral downward. Many factors seemed to conspire against the once high-flying enterprise. For one thing, the die-cast collectibles industry became extremely soft, dramatically impacting virtually every company in the field, including The Franklin Mint.

The market became saturated with die-cast product as many companies tried to take advantage of the appetite for die-cast. Corporate licenses—including Harley-Davidson—were acquired and marketed by a number of die-cast competitors. Soon, such potent franchises as the Coca-Cola series began to show diminishing results. Also, the prices of Matchbox Collectibles products were on the rise, so the competitive advantage that gave Matchbox Collectibles its early impetus began to deteriorate.

The company found that its ads weren't attracting the volume of collectors needed to justify the investment. And, while existing Matchbox Collectibles customers—which reached a peak of about 600,000—still made most direct-mail promotions profitable, losses in other areas began to take their toll.

There was one notable exception. In the year 2000, Matchbox Collectibles issued a series of World War II planes. The timing was superb as Americans were renewing interest in World War II, in part based on a blockbuster movie. The response—from both new and existing Matchbox Collectibles collectors—was

phenomenal. The company had proven that you could still achieve strong performance in an otherwise soft collectibles market.

However, the success of the World War II series was greatly offset by many other models and series that did not do well. Early in 2001, Mattel decided to shut down the Matchbox Collectibles mail-order business. Models and series would still be available via the Internet. By then, the specialty-retail channel had also declined significantly.

Mattel, which had experienced far greater diversity in other areas—including the acquisition and eventual sale of The Learning Company—was focused on strengthening its core retail toy businesses. Although the company still owned successful direct businesses, including The Pleasant Company and the Barbie® direct operation, Mattel had also seen how Hot Wheels hadn't performed well in the direct channel. Tellingly, a once formidable Mattel competitor—Hasbro—started a direct collectibles business in 1999, only to shut it down in early 2001, at about the time that Matchbox Collectibles began dramatically decelerating its direct channel activity.

Although Matchbox Collectibles seemed to suffer from the same forces that hurt other die-cast collectibles at the turn of the twenty-first century, its achievements will endure as important milestones in the history of Matchbox. The enterprise proved that the same company that could create toys for kids that grew into adult collectibles could also create replicas that would satisfy the most demanding die-cast collector.

"The period from 1994 to 1999 was one of the most exciting for Matchbox," says Ken Hill, Mattel senior product designer. "Perhaps never before had a die-cast collectibles company come so far so fast. Most important of all, we developed the best die-cast Matchbox models ever. Their legacy will live on well into the twenty-first century."

191

Promotional Models with Limited Distribution

1946 Dodge 4x4 Power Wagon, 7th Matchbox
Hershey Toy Show (quantity 210)

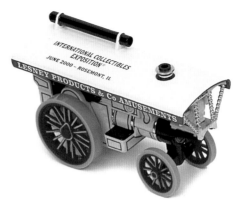

1905 Fowler B6 Showmans Engine, I.C.E.,
Rosemont, IL (quantity 400)

1929 Morris Light Van, Antiques Roadshow, Going
Live (quantity 24)

1937 Cord 812 Sedan, Matchbox Collectibles
(Australia) Conference (quantity 50)

1912 Ford Model T Van, See's Candy
(quantity 3,000)

1938 Lincoln Zephyr,
Ashley Avery Father's Day Event (quantity 76)

1926 Ford Model TT Van,
Jenny Kee (quantity 1,000)

1941 Chevrolet Pickup,
Hope Springs 2000 (quantity 45)

1955 Chevrolet 3100 Pickup, 8th Matchbox
Hershey Toy Show (quantity 210)

1953 Ford F-11 Fire Truck, Tucson Toy
Fair 2001 (quantity 100)

1970 Chevrolet Chevelle SS454,
Matchbox Collectibles Meeting 1999
(quantity 25)

1940 Ford Pickup, 6th Matchbox
Hershey Toy Show (quantity 280)

Promotional Models with Limited Distribution

1926 Ford Model TT Van, Pro Hart
(quantity 1,000)

1928 Austin 7 Van, F.A.O. Schwartz,
Set of Four Christmas (1995) Ornaments
(quantity 7,500 sets)

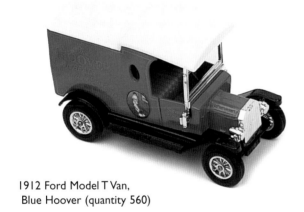

1912 Ford Model T Van,
Blue Hoover (quantity 560)

1928 Austin 7 Van, F.A.O. Schwartz,
Set of Four Christmas (1995) Ornaments
(quantity 7,500 sets)

1970 Chevrolet Chevelle SS454,
Mattel Meeting 1998 (quantity 50)

1911 Ford Model T Car,
Matchbox Collectors Club
(quantity 900)

1928 Austin 7 Van, F.A.O. Schwartz,
Set of Four Christmas (1995) Ornaments
(quantity 7,500 sets)

1981 Morris Pantechnicon,
I.C.E., Atlanta, GA (quantity 300)

1928 Austin 7 Van, F.A.O. Schwartz,
Set of Four Christmas (1995) Ornaments
(quantity 7,500 sets)

1955 Chevrolet 3100 Wrecker Truck,
Orlando Toy Fair 2001
(quantity 120)

1918 Crossley Truck, U.K. Matchbox Club
(quantity 930)

1907 UNIC Taxi, I.C.E., Long Beach, CA
(quantity 500)

1928 Austin 7 Vans:
This set of four vans was issued for Christmas 1994, the first time Models of Yesteryear were produced specifically as Christmas tree ornaments.

197

1939 Bedford

1937 GMC Van

1956 Mack B-95

MATCHBOX Q&A

Q: For which USA TV series did Matchbox secure the rights to produce die-cast vehicles, including the MB111 Snorkel Fire Engine and MB113 Police Launch?

A: Code Red.

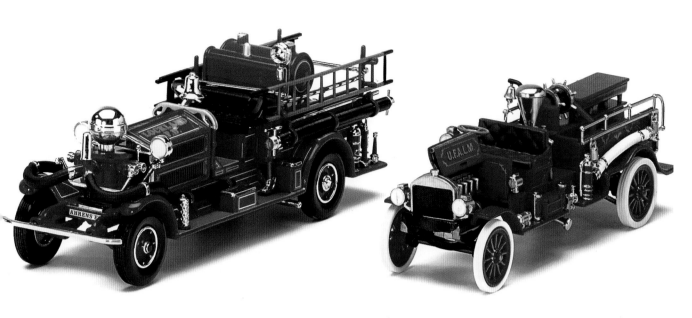

1927 Ahrrens-Fox N-S-4

1911 Mack Fire Pumper

1941 Chevy Military Fire Truck

MATCHBOX® Q&A

Q: What town or fire-company name appears on the YFE02/B Land Rover Fire Engine? In what country is the town located?

A: Londonderry, Australia.

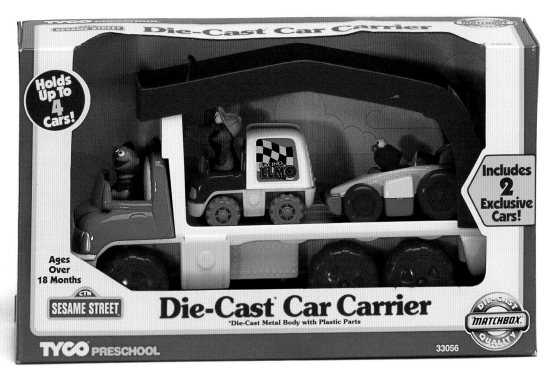

Big Bird's Fire Truck

Elmo's Cement
Truck

Bert 's Tow Truck

Cookie Monster School Bus

Cookie Monster School Bus

Ernie's Police Car

Elmo's Taxi   Zoe's Sports Car   Telly's Front-end Loader

Elmo's Sports Car   Zoe's Sports Car   Ernie's Cement Truck

Sesame Street, 1997

Big Bird Buggy

Oscar's Garbage Truck

Grover's Helicopter

Ernie's Dump Truck

Oscar's Garbage Truck

Big Bird's Delivery Truck

Big Bird Mail Truck

Cookie Monster Airplane

Elmo's Train

Elmo's Dump Truck

Ernie's Buggy

Baby Bear Buggy

203

Peterbilt Semi, rare Tyco
special limited issue

1939 Peterbilt Semi, Campbell's Soup

Kenworth W-900 Tanker Shell

DAF Space Cab, Scuderia Ferrari

16 Mattel and Matchbox Move Forward in the New Millennium

Although Matchbox Collectibles represented a potent sales engine for the Matchbox brand in the nineties, even at its peak it was a very small piece of the Mattel pie. The world's largest toy company by far, Mattel's sales have been between $4 billion and $5 billion annually for a number of years.

Barbie is still the best-selling fashion doll in the world. Hot Wheels is still the largest selling die-cast brand. The Fisher-Price® brand is the leader in infant and preschool toys. And the American Girl® line of dolls and accessories are still very popular among girls. Mattel launched the new Diva Startz product line as well, with very positive results.

Other successful Mattel brands include Fisher-Price Little People® and Mattel markets licensed Harry Potter® and Max Steel® toys. The company has also moved aggressively into games, as well as educational and other software.

And Mattel still has a formidable Matchbox brand. Speaking of Mattel and Matchbox, they were born two years apart.

Mattel's Roots Begin Before Matchbox

Mattel was born two years before Lesney Products, in 1945. Just as Lesney didn't start out making toys, neither did Mattel. Elliott and Ruth Handler joined with co-founder Harold Matson and began making picture frames in a workshop in the Handlers' garage. And guess what—the name Mattel was created in much the same way as Lesney and other toy giants. Mattel was formed from the first three letters of the name Matson and the first three letters of the name Elliott Odell of Mattel. On the side, he began making dollhouse furniture from the scraps left over from making picture frames. After Matson was bought out, the Handlers—encouraged by Matson's success with dollhouses—began crafting toys. And the rest, as they say, is history.

In 1947, Mattel introduced "Uke-A-Doodle," its first musical toy line. Incorporated the following year, Mattel began advertising toys through the *Mickey Mouse Club* TV show in 1955, revolutionizing the way toys were marketed. The Burp Gun, an automatic cap gun, was introduced the same year.

Just as Jack Odell created the first "Matchbox" model for his daughter, Ruth Handler was inspired by her daughter's fascination with cutout paper dolls, leading to Handler's creation of Barbie®, which made her debut in 1959. The world's most famous doll was named after Ruth Handler's daughter.

Mattel went public in 1960. A year later, Barbie was joined by Ken® who was named, not surprisingly, after the Handlers' son. Mattel made the Fortune 500 in 1965 with sales over $100 million, and the company introduced its first educational preschool toy—See 'N Say®—the same year.

1968: A Year of Triumph and Pitfalls

Then, in 1968, Mattel made a profound and lasting impact on the die-cast toy industry with the introduction of those bold, bright, and outrageous Hot Wheels.

As discussed at length in Chapter 7, Hot Wheels almost killed Matchbox, but both survived and thrived. Although Hot Wheels was an instant sensation, Mattel made a number of questionable acquisitions that caused the company to lose focus—and money. These dubious deals included a pet-products company, a motion-picture production company, and Ringling Brothers and Barnum & Bailey Circus.

In 1972, the company went through a restructuring. The Handlers—Mattel's founders—left the company in 1975. Mattel dove into the rapidly growing electronic game market with Intellivision in 1977. By 1983, the company reported a loss of $394 million and sold off its unprofitable non-toy businesses to focus on its money-making toy lines, which included Masters of the Universe®, led by He-Man®, a product line so successful, it briefly eclipsed Barbie in sales.

Just as Universal began developing Disney-licensed toys after acquiring Matchbox, Mattel revived its relationship with Disney in 1988 and introduced infant and preschool toys based on Disney characters. The agreement was expanded to include films and to encompass other product forms, including dolls, games, and puzzles.

Mattel Gains Market Dominance Through Strategic Acquisitions

Mattel's many acquisitions during the eighties and nineties were based on its focused strategy, which was to become the world leader in toys and games. Mattel bought Corolle S.A., a French manufacturer of collector dolls; Corgi, the British die-cast model company (see Chapter 12); Aviva Sports, which makes sport toys; and International Games, Inc. Mattel then merged with Fisher-Price in 1993 and gained a leader in infant and preschool toys, as well as such accessories as nursery monitors and strollers. To further strengthen its family of toy brands, Mattel bought Kransco in 1994 and got Power Wheels®, Hula-Hoop®, and Frisbee®.

In 1995, Mattel acquired the rights to manufacture and distribute Cabbage Patch Kids®, one of the most successful doll concepts of all time. Tickle Me® Elmo generated over $300 million in sales in its first two years. Mattel also entered into a lucrative licensing agreement with Nickelodeon, the most popular children's TV network. Mattel began making toys based on the popular Nickelodeon characters.

Meanwhile, Hot Wheels entered the Winston Cup racing arena and sponsored a car driven by Kyle Petty. Soon Hot Wheels was marketing racing toys, collectible cars, and other licensed products targeted to racing fans who have made NASCAR the world's fastest-growing spectator sport.

Then, in 1996, Mattel took a giant step toward toy industry dominance with its acquisition of Tyco. Mattel added more muscle to its core strengths by obtaining the primary license for *Sesame Street*, by gaining solid infant and preschool brands, and by rounding out its growing "wheels" business. In addition to getting Tyco® R/C (radio-control cars), Mattel now had Matchbox and Matchbox Collectibles.

MATCHBOX® Q&A

Q: What was the latest million-plus unit production quantity for Matchbox?
A: The Target VW Concept 1 model given away by Target Stores in the USA at Thanksgiving, 2000.

MATCHBOX® Trivia

Have you ever wondered why the Anheuser-Busch symbol is an "A" and an eagle and not an "A" and a "B"? Some say that the eagle represents Adolphus Busch's great entrepreneurial vision.

Matchbox SuperFast Models

Mercedes-Benz
E-430 Wagon

King Tow, 2001

Truck Camper, 1999

Airport Fire Tender, 1992

Pontiac Firebird Ram Air, 1997

2000 Corvette Convertible, 2001

Dodge Viper RT/IO, 1994

BMW 328I, 2000

Dodge Viper GTS Coupe, 1997

Dodge Viper RT/IO, 1994

Volkswagen 1967 Delivery Van, 2000

Volkswagen 1967 Delivery Van, 2000

Mercedes-Benz A-Class, 2000

Volkswagen Transporter, 1999

Volkswagen Concept 1 Convertible, 2000

Volkswagen Concept 1 1996

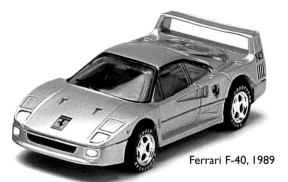

Ferrari F-40, 1989

1962 Volkswagen Sedan, 1999

Formula One Racer, 1994

Mustang Convertible, 1999

17 The Recent Evolution of Matchbox

To understand where Matchbox is today and where the brand seems to be headed, it's enlightening to see how the die-cast models sold in the mass retail channel have evolved over recent years. And, to fully understand this evolution, we have to go back to the acquisition of Matchbox by Tyco.

When Tyco acquired Matchbox in 1992, the biggest markets for Matchbox were the United Kingdom and Western Europe, followed by the U.S., Australia, and other parts of the world. Under the influence of Tyco—an American company with the U.S. as its principal market—product design began to take on a more American flavor.

More American cars and decoration found their way into the Matchbox 1-75 line, which required an investment in more new tooling than in previous years. This was, in part, to compete with Hot Wheels. Even though Hot Wheels was primarily an American brand and Matchbox was clearly international, Tyco wanted to give Matchbox more presence in the U.S. marketplace. The investment seemed to pay off. Matchbox sales increased in 1994 and 1995 after many new models were added to the line.

"Tyco wanted us to go after Hot Wheels," says Rich Plescia," a Mattel senior designer. "There was renewed emphasis on SuperFast and getting the cars to work well on tracks. We redesigned the wheels so that the cars ran on the outer edges, not on the entire wheel. We also looked at the axles, because the smaller the axle, the less resistance and the faster the model goes. We made the axles as thin as we could. The result was that Matchbox cars became faster than previous SuperFast and Laser Wheels."

The competition with Hot Wheels even influenced packaging. Matchbox packaging had utilized blue. Then, when Hot Wheels started using blue, Matchbox began using shades of orange. Over the past several years, the color sensation has shifted from bright orange and yellow to a redder orange.

What Happens When Rivals Become Friends?

When Mattel acquired Tyco and the Matchbox brand, the company faced a tricky challenge: how to differentiate its two world-famous die-cast brands: Hot Wheels and Matchbox. In general, Mattel has done this by positioning Hot Wheels under the theme of "Speed, Power, Performance." Hot Wheels models are generally based on racing of one sort or another—from the track to the drag strip. The models are often replicas of customized vehicles as well, not conventional street vehicles. Moreover, Hot Wheels graphics and colors tend to be, shall we say, electric.

While Matchbox has been associated with racing, this theme was fairly short-lived. For a time, Matchbox had a relationship with White Rose Collectibles, which produced models of NASCAR race cars for Matchbox. But this was an aberration. For the most part, Matchbox has been known for replicating cars, vans, trucks, rigs, planes, and other vehicles that have been part of mainstream life. While this tradition is currently undergoing a very interesting transition, Matchbox has been associated with authenticity and realism for the past fifty years.

In Chapter 9, we saw that senior product designer Ken Hill began creating more elaborate models that were more intricate than conventional die-cast toys. That was in 1989. By the mid-nineties, Hill's "World Class" series gave way to an even more advanced series called the "Premiere Collection." These models were distinguished by vacuum-metallized wheels and hubs and detailed interiors. Even less toylike than World Class, the Premiere Collection now bears the Matchbox Collectibles brand.

In 1995, still determined to compete with Hot Wheels, Matchbox began introducing bolder paint schemes into the 1-75 series. The Ferrari F-40 sported an eye-catching crackle paint scheme and the Dodge Challenger was tampo printed—which is similar to hand painting—to create an exciting look. The black paint has a spidery look against the solid yellow background. And Matchbox began to move outside its traditional mode of replicating real vehicles, with animal cars. Like the Lesney "Rola-matics" that first appeared in the early seventies, the animal cars had parts that moved as the vehicle rolled, such as the Rotwheeler, with a dog's jaw that opens and closes.

The Spirit of Innovation Continually Drives Matchbox Design

Matchbox chalked up another first in 1997 with its new "Inaugurals." This series was created as a way to justify the cost of new tooling. Each model was crafted as part of a very limited production run and each featured a clear coating over a raw die-cast body to prevent tarnishing and to meet safety standards. Every Inaugurals model had the same interior as the later, decorated models. And each came in a blue window box. By the way, the Boeing 757 was the only plane in this series, and it is both rare and difficult to find today.

In 1998, Matchbox introduced its First Editions, which represented an advance in wheel design. Each three-piece wheel included its own hub. While most models were replicas of actual road vehicles, "First Editions," included animal cars. Also, color schemes were more attuned to what kids wanted—a cool, trendy look.

In the following year, 1999, Matchbox began to create "generic" models as well. These models didn't bear the graphics of any company, and the lack of licensing fees meant that they could be sold at lower price points, providing better value to kids and collectors.

The year 1999 was also noteworthy because Mattel decided that the Matchbox 1-75 series should have 100 models instead of seventy-five. Although this decision has since been reversed—preserving the sanctity of the most important series Matchbox ever developed—it meant that the year 1999 would see a surge in new Matchbox tooling. "We developed twenty-four new tools that year," says Jim Dickinson, senior designer, "twelve generic and twelve licensed. And, in many ways, we got back to basics, giving customers the qualities they had always prized in Matchbox." These included opening doors on cars and a pop-up camper, fun features geared to kids.

"We also became more responsive to the different needs of our markets," Dickinson says. "So we created unique lines for three markets—Germany, the U.K., and Australia." Each market could choose from a list of twenty vehicles and models were decorated to appeal to people in those countries. "For example, the Brits would ask for the Union Jack to appear on British cars, and Germany chose a Mercedes for a police car because German police drive Mercedes. We made a Mercedes E-430 station wagon for Germany, a model we would never make for the U.S."

Matchbox was getting back to its core strength as an international brand capable of appealing to specific tastes around the globe.

Rescue Is the Underlying Theme of Today's Matchbox

While the most dominant theme of Hot Wheels is racing—described by its mantra of speed, power, and performance—the theme that has defined Matchbox in recent years is Matchbox to the Rescue™. Another tagline that captures the spirit of Matchbox today is: "Own the Vehicles Your Heroes Drive," which describes a line dominated by vehicles driven by the people kids most admire.

In addition to the obvious choices—police and fire—there are vehicles operated by workers kids see in their neighborhoods, such as the snow groomer and street cleaner. A child might look up to construction workers, teachers, or their parents; all these "heroes," and more, are honored in Matchbox models and sets.

Among the latest Matchbox innovations, "one of the most difficult models to develop was our post-office van," Jim Dickinson muses. "It took almost a year just to get the license. We had to get approval from Grumman who owns the license on the van and Grumman, in turn, licenses the design to the U.S. Postal Service. We had to get their approval too."

Matchbox Steps Up the Pace in 2001

For 2001, Matchbox developed thirty-five new tools, which represents a very high level of commitment to its rescue theme. The new line features an array of new construction vehicles and many generic designs created by the in-house design team.

"These include models with a completely new look for us," says senior product designer Jim Carty. Take the King Tow™ truck, for example. "This is one of a new generation of Matchbox models that balance realism with a look designed to impress kids. It has a beefier front and more detailed towing apparatus than our previous tow truck. It's also more intricate, with such details as a crowbar and work gloves."

The new look also features "punchier, brighter, more contemporary" decoration, says designer Jim Carty. "The new look can be found in everything from boats and hovercraft to radar trucks. And the look is carried through other Matchbox lines, including our popular play sets and the Rescue Net™ large-truck line."
But the beauty of the latest Matchbox models is

more than skin deep. "In addition to designing more dramatic looking vehicles, we have also incorporated more moving parts," says Carty. "The weather radar truck comes equipped with a radar dish that goes up and down and rotates in a complete circle. The police-style Hummer has a roof that flips open to reveal an ATV. And the Road Roller® Paver not only rolls, but its back end pivots, just like the real thing."

"It's the best of the old and new," says Jim Pisors, marketing director of Matchbox Collectibles. "We're getting back to many of the features that intrigued us when we bought Matchbox as kids. But we're also updating the look and advancing the quality to appeal to the kids of today."

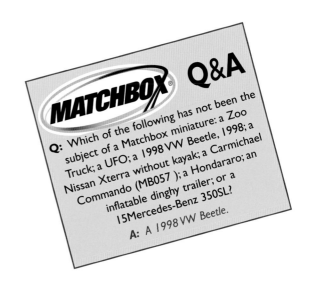

MATCHBOX® Q&A

Q: Which of the following has not been the subject of a Matchbox miniature: a Zoo Truck; a UFO; a 1998 VW Beetle, 1998; a Nissan Xterra without kayak; a Carmichael Commando (MB057); a Hondararo; an inflatable dinghy trailer; or a 15Mercedes-Benz 350SL?

A: A 1998 VW Beetle.

Four Premiere Collectibles

1964 1/2 Mustang, 1999

2000 Thunderbird, 1999

Blimp, 2000

1957 Corvette, 1999

Premiere Collectibles

International Fire Pumper

Airport Crash Tender Fire Truck

1969 Camaro Convertible SS 396

1968 Mustang Cobra/Jet Fastback

2000 Chevy Suburban Fire Chief

Corvette Sting-Ray III Concept Car

2000 Chevy Suburban Military Police

USAF Flight Crew Transport

1971 Camaro Z-28

Snorkel Fire Truck, Seaside Fire Department

Ford Crown Victoria Police Car, New Jersey

Dodge Challenger

Matchbox SuperFast Models

Land Rover Discovery, 2001

U.S. Mail Truck, 2000

Jeep Liberty, 2001

Street Streak, 1996

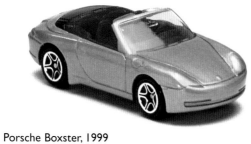

Porsche Boxster, 1999

Lotus Elise, 2000

Jaguar XJ, 1998

BMW 3 Series Coupe, 2000

4-Wheeler ATV, 1999

Ford Box Van, 1999

BMW Z-3, 1997

Ford Focus, 2000

4x4 Open Back Truck, 1982

Porsche Boxster, 1999

Audi TT Roadster, 2000

BMW 3 Series Coupe, 2000

Matchbox First Editions

The first unpainted castings are in the outside columns

Kenworth T-2000, cab unpainted

Kenworth T-2000, cab painted

Ford F-150 Pickup

Ford F-150 Pickup

1968 Mustang Fastback Cobra/Jet

1968 Mustang Fastback Cobra/Jet

1997 Jaguar XK-8 Convertible

1997 Jaguar XK-8 Convertible

Chevy Tahoe

Chevy Tahoe

1957 Chevy Bel Air Convertible

1957 Chevy Bel Air Convertible

1955 Chevy Bel Air Two-door Hardtop

1955 Chevy Bel Air Two-door Hardtop

1957 Corvette Roadster

1957 Corvette Roadster

Matchbox First Editions

The first unpainted castings are in the outside columns

Ford F-150 Pickup

Ford F-150 Pickup

Dodge Viper GTS Coupe

Dodge Viper GTS Coupe

1970 Boxx 302 Mustang Fastback

1970 Boxx 302 Mustang Fastback

Dodge Concept Car

Dodge Concept Car

1956 Ford Pickup

1956 Ford Pickup

1957 Chevy Bel Air Two-door Hardtop

1957 Chevy Bel Air Two-door Hardtop

1970 Chevy El Camino Pickup

1970 Chevy El Camino Pickup

1999 Porsche Boxster

1999 Porsche Boxster

Three MCI Coach Buses, 1999: *I Dream of Jeannie*

Scooby-Doo

Walt Disney, the first Convoy Scale bus ever issued

Daffy Duck

Road Runner

Bugs Bunny

Tazmanian Devil

Wile E. Coyote

Ford F-350, Dually Texaco

Chevy Suburban, Mesa Fire Chief, 1-1/24 scale

Ford Sedan Delivery, Campbell's, 1-1/18 scale

KME Mini-Pumper Ford-F350 Chassis

2002 Jeep Liberty

Bellevue Police VW Concept, "D.A.R.E."

Jeepster Concept Vehicle

Concept VW, Only at TRU

227

Dodge Power Wagon, 1946

Frightliner C.O.E. Container Truck, Beefeater Gin,
1:58 scale, from Collectibles

Dodge Power Wagon, Brush Truck, 1946

Airplane Collectibles

P-51 Mustang

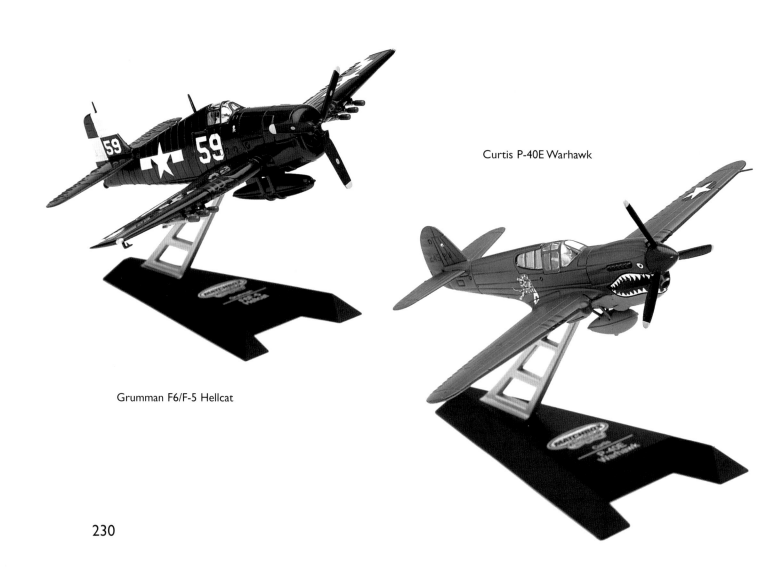

Curtis P-40E Warhawk

Grumman F6/F-5 Hellcat

Chance-Vought F4U-1A Corsair

P-38 Lockheed Lightning

Supermarine MK-1A Spitfire

Military Collectibles

Panzer IV F-1 2000

Sherman M4A3

Sherman M4A3

1945 Willys Jeep

Opposite page:

The Matchbox room of a typical "dedicated collector"; even the window is obscured by cabinets! However, daylight is the true collector's biggest enemy since ultraviolet rays discolor both paint finishes and self-colored plastics. Note that the models are displayed on the shelves diagonally, to conserve space, and gaps are left for models that are still being sought.

1946 Dodge Power Wagon Firetruck, Brush Unit, 2002

Chef Boyardee Mail-in Promotion (USA), 1985

Convoy Scania Tanker,
Cadbury's Fudge

Kit Kat, British Promotion:
Red Ford Transit Van

White Volvo Container Truck

McDonald's Happy Meal Promotion, April 2002,
with six state cars: Texas, Ohio, New York, North Carolina, Illinois, and Washington

MATCHBOX Trivia

Because of the difficulty the Japanese have with the letter "R," Ronald McDonald is called Donald McDonald in Japan. In China, he's called McDonald Suk Suk or Uncle McDonald. Ronald McDonald first appeared on TV in 1963, played by Willard Scott.

MATCHBOX Trivia

On the day that McDonald's opened in Kuwait City in 1994, the line for the drive-in was seven miles long.

Models of Yesteryear, 1930 Model A Ford Van, OXO Beef Cubes, U.K.

18 Matchbox Celebrates Its 50th in Style

The foreword of this book briefly mentions some of the ways Mattel is celebrating the 50th anniversary of Matchbox. For the Matchbox 1-75 series, twenty-four new models have been developed and the first 10,000 of each will bear the 50th anniversary medallion. In addition, the "Matchbox® Across America 50th Birthday Series" line honors fifty years of Matchbox history with fifty models, one representing each of the fifty states. Again, only the first 10,000 of each will be decorated with the 50th anniversary logo.

The Matchbox Across America 50th Birthday Series line is not only a milestone for Matchbox, but for the design team as well. "Whenever possible, we tried to marry the vehicle to the state," says Jim Carty. So there's a pony trailer for Kentucky, a Ford Model T for Michigan, a dairy truck for Wisconsin, and a golf cart for South Carolina. "The decoration depicts something the state is famous for, such as oranges for Florida and a boat with a crab motif for Maryland." Each vehicle is sold with a miniature replica of the state's license plate. Each license plate bears the state abbreviation and the sequence of each state joining the union. So Delaware's plate says: DE001. Moreover, each license plate is separate from the model.

"We've decided to divide up the U.S. into four regions," says Ira Rubien of Mattel, with a different color license plate for each region. "If you get five models from that region, you get a bonus car. If you collect all fifty, you'll get a car and license plate for Washington, D.C. There is also a separate car for Puerto Rico."

There is also a "collector board," which is very similar to the cardboard album used to collect coins. There are slots for all the miniature license plates. In addition, "there is a 50th anniversary carrying case that holds all fifty cars and license plates," says Rubien. "And, at the end of the year, there will be a 50th anniversary fifty pack with a custom display case."

For the international markets, Mattel has created international "birthday hunt vehicles." "There are four models with commemorative decoration," says Rubien, "a Ford Model A,

1962 VW Beetle, fire truck, and London taxi." Mattel is also providing exclusive multi-packs for certain retailers. Each one consists of two cars and a collector guide that describes all fifty cars in the series. "We're also getting a North American multi pack with two state cars plus a USA car, two with a Canada car, and two with a Mexico car."

Kids are getting free Matchbox 50th anniversary toy cars in the McDonald's Happy Meals program, which consists of six models from the Matchbox Across America 50th Birthday Series line. And there is a traveling road show that is making 300 stops across the U.S., mostly at K Mart and Wal-Mart stores. In other words, Mattel is celebrating the 50th anniversary of its legendary Matchbox brand in grand style.

Matchbox Collectibles: The 50th Anniversary Collection

1923 Mac AC

1939 Bedford
Fire Truck

1953 Ford Fire Truck

KME Mini Pumper

Chevy Suburban Fire Chief

Chevy Impala Fire Chief

2002 Corvette

Ford F-350 Pickup

1933 Ford Street Rod

1964-1/2 Ford Mustang

1967 Volkswagen Van

1955 Chevy Belair Convertible

Dennis Sabre Fire Truck

1962 Volkswagen Sedan

1955 Cadillac Fleetwood

Behind the Scenes with the Unsung Heroes

Whether with a good machine or a memorable artistic performance, the "trick" in bringing any new creation to fruition is making the process appear effortless. Trials, tribulations, sweat, and toil should be invisible to all except the creators.

Just so with the Matchbox product. On the 50th anniversary of Matchbox, it is time to acknowledge the countless individuals who have made vital contributions to the development and evolution of Matchbox designs.

A brief peep behind the curtain reveals designers working to marry the often disparate and seemingly contradictory desires of marketing and sales people. The design process is often complicated by any license holders' requirements. And one must always be conscious of the company's "Product Integrity."

Working with the designers are the engineers who transform the designs into engineering drawings, remembering tooling constrictions, and correctly anticipating the unexpected. Then there are the tool makers who craft the tools with one eye on the drawings and the other on what can be realistically achieved in the manufacturing environment.

While the designers and engineers transform ideas into real products, the packaging team enters and exits the scene at differing points depending upon the subject. Will the packaging structure meet differing world perceptions as to optimum forms of presentation? And, just as importantly, will the structure withstand tests on the rigors of transportation and mishandling? The technological developments in package graphics have continually evolved throughout the history of Matchbox, spurred on by a commitment to remain fresh and new. For example, the decision on the Matchbox logo change in 2001 involved a great many people and considerable discussion and analysis; then, once the design was chosen, the packaging people worked just as hard to give the new look maximum impact.

When it comes to both product and packaging, the key is to satisfy the consumer while also managing the costs. Instrumental in this critical equation are the costing engineers. With fingers dancing over buttons, they calculate the cost implications of a variety of "what if" scenarios, right down to 0.001 in a cost equation.

The project engineers in production are classic examples of ingenious people who are able to make the whole far greater than the sum of the parts. Working against the clock and compressed deadlines and fearing the worst, they take each product concept and somehow wet-nurse it to life.

Product planners who work with the forecasts and orders from marketing and sales possibly know more about trends and performances than anyone else. They are your best friend when it comes to getting product quicker than reality would suggest possible; or they are your nemesis when that forecast you stood by optimistically—or foolishly—results in product writeoffs and financial charge-backs.

New toy planners stare intently into the foggy future and try to chart a development time frame for each and every product brought to market. Theirs is a daunting task. For the calendar year 2001, for example, there were over 1,200 different products produced under the Matchbox brand by Mattel.

The quality-assurance and quality-control personnel in manufacturing slavishly test product to ensure compliance with statutory regulations such as ASTMS for the USA or EN71 for Europe. It is worth noting that the toy industry produces products that are often miniaturized versions of real world vehicles, and toy regulations are a labyrinth seemingly designed to confound Theseus.

Then you have the legal eagles who, naturally, have an opinion about everything and can bring matters to a grinding halt or accelerate rapturous product performance, depending upon the scenario.

Much of the above takes place for the initial production. There are mountains of paperwork to complete for export documentation and certifications; Bills of Lading for shipment; customs papers for importation; trucking documents for onward shipment; warehousing—an art all to itself—and then distribution as the final link in a chain that can stretch many months and make its way through, literally, hundreds of hands.

If one were to try to compile a list of individuals involved in the many and various functions of bringing a Matchbox product from the drawing board to the store near you, the list would be endless. Each deserves his or her name in print, but the list might require a book bigger than the one you hold in your hands. Even if I were to attempt such a list, I would be nagged by the fear of forgetting someone, which would be quite inevitable.

Suffice it to say that this book is a reflection of product conceived and brought to reality, for good or bad, with determination or by accident, by people who, with their Matchbox product, wanted to create something different.

They succeeded. Frequently. Often brilliantly.

They know who they are. They know we are grateful to them.

Simon Iredale
October 2001

Everything You Ever Wanted to Know About the Matchbox Numbering Logic

Matchbox 1-75 series (MB1-75):

Each time Matchbox intentionally made a different vehicle by tool set and/or by decoration, the item was officially recognized with a different code.

If the vehicle tool set changed, the number would change. If only the decoration changed, then only the alphabetical code after the number changed.

For example, the very first "MB" was the Aveling Barford Road Roller (in green). This was originally numbered as MB1. In 1956, the color was changed to light green. At this juncture, the alphabetical coding arrived to designate color or decoration changes. The Aveling in 1956 officially became MB1B. Two years later, it changed again and became MB1C.

In 1967, the Aveling Barford was replaced with a Mercedes Truck. This was given the designation of MB1E. Why MB1, you ask?

With rare exceptions, the numbers have never been marketed with a number higher than MB75. The decision for the choice of MB1-75 is one really lost in time, though it was thought to be a marketing/sales decision. In any case, when you limit yourself to using only seventy-five numbers and a vehicle is to be replaced, the incoming vehicle takes the number of the outgoing one.

This is why, for example, MB1 can have subject matter ranging from an Aveling Barford Road Roller or a Mercedes Truck to a Dodge Challenger or a Jaguar XJ6.

When Matchbox was purchased by Universal and production was moved to the Far East, the manufacturing numbering of tool plans bothered some people. To a logistical planner in this complex world, you "cannot" have more than one subject matter for MB1. Hence, the Matchbox manufacturing numbering principles underwent a change and the system established in 1983–1984 remains in place. The general public does not see this system but it is what the factory works by. Manufacturing knows that if there are more than seventy-five models, then you have to break free from the marketing straight-jacket of 1-75 and have MB76 and upwards. At present, there are nearly 600 MB numbers.

If this is clear so far, this is where the layers of complexity start piling up. There is more than one MB1-75 range in the world at any time. This is because one market believes it cannot sell the same range of vehicles and/or colored vehicles that another market can. In the late 1990s, the complexity had exploded to five different MB1-75 ranges between the Americas, the United Kingdom, Germany, Australia, and the Rest of the World (ROW). Although the five markets have elements in common, significant differences exist. As a result, the factory could be making five different number MB20s at the same

An early steamshovel (right) is placed next to a more contemporary example.

time for a variety of countries or regions. This further explains why Universal introduced a new manufacturing number system in the eighties.

The decoration code after an MB number indicates the version. A letter is used so as not to confuse the vehicle tool set number with the decoration code. When vehicles and their decorations are used for purposes other than the classic MB1-75, they get different decoration codes.

For example, the 2002 line in the Americas has sequence MB#5 Chevrolet Impala Police. This is MB number MB420. The decoration is the third version in MB1-75 and is therefore given the decoration code C. This gives us MB420/C. The MB420/C is also used in the 2002 ten-pack gift set which is a repackaged selection of models from MB1-75. The Rest of the World (ROW) sequence MB#5 isn't the Chevrolet Impala Police car, but a Porsche Boxster, which is MB356. The 2002 ROW version is the fourth decoration type in MB1-75 and is therefore decoration code D, resulting in MB356/D.

When the Chevrolet Impala Police or Porsche Boxster—or any of the other MB vehicles—are used outside of MB1-75 (or in packs where the MB1-75 decoration is used), they get a completely different—though still alphabetical—decoration code. For example, the MB420 is also used in the five-pack Patrol & Protect™ in 2002. Here, the full manufacturing code is

MB420/SE. The two letters, SE, differentiate this product from the MB1-75 series, which always uses only one letter as a decoration code.

Manufacturing variants sometimes occur, including the incorrect combination of parts. If the factory is simultaneously making the MB420 Chevrolet Impala Police car for the 2002 MB1-75 Americas line alongside the same car as another version for the five-pack Patrol & Protect set, the different colored interiors could be accidentally swapped for a limited number of pieces. Such variants do not receive different decoration codes because they are unintentional. The number of variants in the past fifteen years or so has dropped as the level of quality control has increased.

Before any production occurs, there is testing on the initial run of each of several thousand models. This involves testing for heavy elements, pull tests, drop tests, sharp-point testing, and numerous other safety issues, roll and general function, as well as overall workmanship, which includes correctness against the signed off "final engineering pilot" samples. During the vehicle's production life cycle, there are frequent, random tests on given lot sizes. Simply put, there is much less chance of a variant.

If there is a wheel style or size change and this is the only adjustment to the vehicle, it does not get a new MB or decoration code. If the MB420/C wheel set is different from the

MB420/B version, that is designated on the decoration-code master-color matrix and plan. If, for whatever reason (such as a tool breakdown), the wheels change during the production of the MB420/C and revert back to the MB420/B type, that will not be recorded by a change to /D.

Matchbox does change the MB number if the tool set changes in parts usage for a finished good. For example, the MB304 is the Ford Crown Victoria Police car, with a low profile light bar on the roof. If the design department wishes to change this to a "V"-shaped–style light bar such as the one first used on the MB379, then the MB304 code changes as well, in this case to MB459.

Convoys

"Convoy" (a.k.a. Super Rigs) is a product line featuring an MB-size cab or tractor and a trailer. The Convoy numbering system works on the following principle: take the MB cab number plus the trailer number for the next numerical sequence Convoy number known as CY.

Therefore, the MB202 Mack with the CY009 Forty-Foot Container is CY027 and the MB202 with the CY018 Double Container trailer is CY028.

How do we number the MCI Bus, which is only one vehicle as opposed to the cab and trailer combination of all other Convoy vehicles? In this case, the decoration system functions as it does with the 1-75 series. All other Matchbox die-cast models follow the Matchbox 1-75 series numbering system as well, except for "Super Kings"; if a Super Kings vehicle consists of a cab and trailer, it follows the Convoy numbering logic.

Models of Yesteryear

The famed Models of Yesteryear line is no exception; it follows the Matchbox 1-75 series numbering system. However, as with the 1-75 models, there used to be a marketing limit: in this case, no marketed numbers above YY30. This was handled in the same fashion as with the 1-75 series (see above).

More recently, the numbering process was complicated. A model that had been a Models of Yesteryear was designated a Dinky or vice-versa. But manufacturing used the original designation in its numbering. In other words, manufacturing considered a Models of Yesteryear a Models of Yesteryear, even if Marketing labeled it a Dinky. Marketing also wished to apply a series code to Models of Yesteryear line. An example is YFE, "Yesteryear Fire Engines." The YFE was the marketing code and manufacturing used the YY tool number, changing the decoration code as necessary. However, it soon became apparent that the YFE items would have new and unique tooling. So manufacturing used the marketing code for unique vehicle elements.

Mattel

When Mattel acquired Tyco and the Matchbox brand, this complex numbering system was new to Mattel. Mattel wanted Matchbox to operate under the Mattel coding culture. This was a computer-generated, next-available number system. Yet marketing, especially with the direct-mail portion of collectibles, wanted to retain some element of the Matchbox numbering.

All Matchbox product is now designed, developed, and ordered in the same manner as, say, Hot Wheels, when it comes to numbering. However, there is an efficiency in the Matchbox system. It is much simpler to recognize an alpha-numerical code as a given product (or range) than it is an all numeral one. The Matchbox system is still used as an adjunct to the Mattel digital code throughout the development and production cycle of a product. That's because, quite simply, it works.

Simon Iredale
October 2001

Three examples of firetrucks from Matchbox's early days to the present

The Matchbox Road Museum

It's located in a town you probably never heard of: Newfield, New Jersey. The population, roughly 1,600, apparently hasn't changed in years. The mayor is also the proud owner of the Matchbox Road Museum, which is celebrating its tenth anniversary in 2002.

He is Everett Marshall, one of the world's leading Matchbox authorities. And, since he began collecting Matchbox vehicles in 1980, he has managed to acquire some 27,000 models. This collection is either Number One or Number Two in the world (the other major collection belongs to Matchbox enthusiast Charlie Mack). The Matchbox Road Museum collection is comprehensive in scope, including early and recent models, the full line from Matchbox Collectibles, and just about everything in between.

Every wall in the museum is lined with Matchbox models, from floor to ceiling. And, while no description could possibly do justice to a collection of such impressive size and scope, here are just a few highlights:

• The museum includes at least one model of every Matchbox casting.

• The world's largest collection of "King Size" rigs (1:43 scale, at least a foot long), including both vintage and recent releases, can be found in the museum. Among the old models is a rig that carried cattle. Among the new

ones is one of Everett Marshall's all-time favorites: the Jack Daniel tractor trailer that was promoted solo. He also likes the smaller Miller Brewing rig that was one of six replicas in the North American Brewmasters Collection.

• The museum houses one of the most comprehensive collections of Matchbox memorabilia, including original product drawings and such non die-cast products as the game "Cascade."

• The museum houses one of the most comprehensive collections of Matchbox memorabilia, including original product drawings and such non–die-cast products as the game "Cascade."

• The museum has every Laser Wheel model and all the Dinky models ever made by Matchbox; the most complete collection of Majors models, including prototypes; an impressive array of electric sets and cars; and a substantial collection of Sky Busters® aircraft.

• The museum houses the world's finest collection of Harley-Davidson motorcycle replicas, and some motorcycle models also have riders.

There are cars, trucks, planes, helicopters, military, and construction vehicles. Sometimes one vehicle—such as a boat or tank—rides atop a trailer pulled by a truck. The museum contains intricate fire engines, police cars, airport-security vehicles, and eighteen-wheelers bearing the names of many of the most prestigious companies and brands in the world—including Federal Express, Oreo, M&M, Pepsi, and Coca-Cola.

Everett Marshall is a shrewd collector who has many one-of-a-kind models and pre-production pieces. There are hand samples on display, including a tractor trailer that was designed for Sears but never went into full production. Some of the prototypes have hand-painted artwork on the side, including one for Langendorf bakery with the slogan "The taste of a simpler day." Among the most unusual attractions are:

• The prototype of The Real Model Limousine (which was never produced) from The Real Model Collection, featuring dolls of such celebrities as Christie Brinkley. This model, which is quite large, is "currently worth about $5,000," says Everett Marshall.

• Everett paid $450 for a vintage Prime Mover with Bulldozer and Trailer, one of the early Lesney models. In 1997, Charlie Mack estimated it was worth between $850 and $1,200.

• A one-of-a-kind Viper model created for the TV show that bears the same name.

• The epoxy prototype of a Harley-Davidson Fat Boy.

• An extremely rare box containing seven smaller Matchbox-size boxes, each containing a Matchbox replica, which was probably given by Du Pont to its customers.

• Y-12 promotional models that were also given by companies to customers, including Bird's Custard Powder, Suze, and Harrods.

• A yellow Lesney Ford GT in 1:64 scale which is "the only one I know exists," says Marshall, "and it's probably worth $400 to $500."

• A vast collection of Matchbox SuperFast models, including dozens of replicas that are among the first that Everett Marshall ever purchased for the museum.

• A very rare Auto Park toy. A child would place a Matchbox model inside and turn the outside wheel and the model would move up in a circular path, just like riding on a Ferris wheel. There are slots for nine cars and various gears in the center that make the mechanism work.

Frequently, many versions of a single model were manufactured over time, each with some slight variation. For example, Everett Marshall has accumulated eight different versions of the "Rescue Helicopter" from the Matchbox 1-75 series with color differences on the tail, cross and skid. An even better example is the MB038 tool (sequence # 38), a Model T Ford. The Matchbox Road Museum has over 400 variants.

Just as there were many versions of individual models, Matchbox also made slight modifications to play sets and repackaged them, extending their life. These include the "Take-Along Play set" garage and a "Car Wash" set. The "Sounds of Service" set, which had a diagnostic center that featured seven diagnostic sounds, was slightly modified to become the soundless "Truck Stop" and then resurrected again with its original name.

The Matchbox Road Museum also includes some unusual and fascinating products developed for foreign markets, such as "View-Master Grand Prix," "which was promoted in Spain or Portugal," says Rich Bart, the museum curator. The product combined a View-Master, slides of racing scenes, four die-cast racers, and a colorful board depicting a race track. "My First Matchbox" was designed to appeal to very young children in the U.K. and Germany in the early nineties. The museum also has a full Australian football series—with team emblems on die-cast Holden models—that was never promoted or produced.

A Boyhood Interest Turns into a Collecting Passion

Everett Marshall began collecting Dinky and Matchbox models as a boy. He remembers going into a store in Ocean City, New Jersey, and buying two Matchbox replicas for 98 cents.

He continued collecting Matchbox right into high school and then resumed his favorite pastime after he was married, convincing himself that he was acquiring the models for his son.

When Everett first began collecting the Matchbox 1-75 series, he discovered something many Matchbox collectors have encountered. "I found 1, then 2 and 3, then I found another 1 that wasn't the same one I had." Everett soon learned that Matchbox used the same numbers, but often issued different replicas using that number. "It took me eight or nine years to get all the models listed in Charlie Mack's book covering models made from 1947 to 1969," says Marshall. The book shows hundreds of models. The Marshalls' basement was beginning to look like a Matchbox museum and, in 1992, Marshall Everett decided that's what he should have.

Through the years, Everett has acquired most of the museum's holdings through collectors with especially large or rare collections and toy shows. And he advises today's collectors to "work your way back, beginning in 1997 with the latest editions from Matchbox Collectibles. If you start at the beginning, you'll never make it, because you'll never find all the models you want." He also says, "collect what you like, because you never know what might appreciate in value and what won't." What is particularly hot in today's collector circles? Everett says that "fire, police, and emergency vehicles are

very popular right now, and have been for several years."

The Matchbox Road Museum publishes a full-color newsletter describing Matchbox secondary market models that collectors may acquire. For more information, contact:

Everett Marshall III, Proprietor
Matchbox Road Museum
17 Pearl Street
Newfield, NJ 08344

Telephone: 1-800-976-7623

Biographies

Leslie Charles Smith

Born on March 6, 1918, Leslie Charles Smith was fascinated by clockwork toys, building bricks, and Meccano toys as a boy. Most of the toys his parents bought for him came from Woolworth's. After his school days, he gained employment at J. Raymond Wilson Co., an exporting company that shipped goods to Europe, Australia, and New Zealand. Initially an office boy, Leslie moved up the ladder to the buying department where he bought carpets and textiles. His employment was interrupted by World War II. At twenty-two years old, he enlisted in the Royal Naval Voluntary Reserve as a Signal Rating. Promoted to the rank of lieutenant, Leslie faced the enemy in the North Sea and he also participated in the Dieppe Raid. From Yarmouth to the Hook of Holland, he patrolled dangerous waters aboard gunboats. He also saw action in North Africa, Salerno, and in both the Sicily and D-Day landings. A few months after his tour of military service ended, Smith reconnected with a fellow soldier who he knew from his school days. He and his chum Rodney Smith would go on to make history together as the founders of the company that created the Matchbox legacy.

Rodney Smith

Rodney Smith was born on August 26, 1917. He served in the Royal Navy as a Petty Officer during World War II. After the war, he worked at an engineering firm called Die Cast and Machine Tools in North London, a company known primarily for manufacturing die-casting equipment. After forming Lesney Products with his old school chum Leslie Smith, Rodney focused on die-casting while Leslie handled sales and book-keeping, and Jack Odell was in charge of product design. Unfortunately, Rodney Smith left Lesney shortly before it began a period of rapid growth. Discouraged by the ban on zinc during the Korean War—which was needed to make die-cast toys—Smith left the firm and floundered in his business dealings. After unsuccessful ventures in breeding chickens, ducks, and pigs, he actually tried extracting weeds from the bottom of the river Thames and selling the weeds to Woolworth's as floral decorations. Then he worked briefly for another die-cast company and, when this didn't pan out for him, he moved to Australia. His former associates lost touch with him and Smith became something of a mystery man. No one seems to know what became of him after he settled in Australia in the fifties.

Fred Bronner

Fred Bronner grew up in a middle-class family in Vienna and received a law degree from the University of Vienna. In 1938, he fled Austria to escape the possibility of Nazi persecution. He lived in Paris and Trinidad before the Bronners moved to the United States in 1945. After seeing an ad promoting Matchbox models in an

English magazine, he sent for samples with the idea of selling Matchbox in the U.S. He founded the Fred Bronner Corporation for this very purpose. And he was instrumental in the phenomenal growth of the Matchbox phenomenon in America. He played a critical role in making Matchbox a household name and the thing to collect for generations of American children.

David C. W. Yeh

Born in Shanghai China, on September 3, 1929, David Yeh grew up in Shanghai and then studied banking and finance at St. John's University. Following in his father's footsteps (Mr. Yeh was a banker), David left school to go to work in Hong Kong's Chekiang First Bank as a trainee. After six years in banking, his father convinced him that there was a great future in plastics. His father got a new job in Hong Kong, so that's where David went as well. Their timing was fortuitous, because China fell to the communists in 1949. By this time, David was selling plastic made in Germany to companies in Hong Kong and he fully understood what his father had told him about the fast growing plastics industry. He then joined the toy company run by Louis Marx and received his apprenticeship in toys directly from the master. Marx told Yeh that the Far East would become the preferred place to produce toys in the future, a prediction that came true in part because Yeh believed it as well. After eight years at the Marx toy company, Yeh launched Universal Doll Dress and

Universal Traders and embarked upon an ambitious career in toys. Through well-timed acquisitions—including Lesney Products and Dinky—and a shrewd business sense, he built a global toy empire. From 1982 to 1992, under the ownership of David Yeh's Universal Group, the Matchbox business expanded and grew throughout the world.

Alex Welch

Born in a Florida Navy base when his father was serving in World War II, Alex Welch was raised in Boston and went to school at Tufts University on a Navy ROTC scholarship. He served four years in the U.S. Marine Corp and left as a Captain. He served in demilitarized zones in both Korea and Vietnam. In 1970, Welch went straight to work for the Gillette Company. He was assigned to the Asia Pacific region for Gillette and became one of their youngest country managers, running the Indonesian market after a two-year training stint in Australia. Welch's children were born in both Singapore and Australia. He proceeded to spend the next twenty years of his business career working for Gillette, Alcoa, and Richardson Vicks/Proctor & Gamble, running significant positions in the Asian markets. He returned to the United States with Mattel, where he was in charge of building Mattel's toy brands, including Barbie and Hot Wheels, into the Asia Pacific region. His responsibilities included a Matchbox factory in India, a joint venture in Japan, and the sales offices that Mattel ran throughout the Asia Pacific region, led by Australia. Welch joined Tyco in 1993 as Vice President/ International, arriving just in time for Tyco's purchase of Matchbox. Welch's markets were the U.K., Mexico, Canada, Australia, and New Zealand, and he inherited Matchbox Collectibles worldwide. Welch worked with many people—including Mike Dukes, Sid Sullivan in the U.K., and planning and logistics people led by Simon Iredale—to develop a highly successful Matchbox Collectibles business. After the purchase of Tyco by Mattel, Welch and a group of international associates formed Toy Traders International (TTI), developing toys for the international market. They were very successful in helping Microsoft launch its $150 Actimates Barney program into the U.K. market. Welch worked briefly for Hasbro, then returned to his private practice, which he's currently enjoying.

Mike Dukes

Mike Dukes was born in New Jersey in August of 1950. At a young age, he and his family moved to suburban Philadelphia, where he has lived ever since. Dukes' first job out of high school was working in the coin-making operations at The Franklin Mint. At that time, The Franklin Mint was predominately a coin-manufacturing company, which later evolved into a diversified collectibles marketing company. Dukes attended night school at the local community college where he focused on marketing. Later, he accepted a management position at The Franklin Mint, where he excelled in sales planning and strategies. After twenty-five years at The Franklin Mint, he accepted the opportunity to build a Matchbox Collectibles business for Tyco Toys. The business was wildly successful, and Dukes moved onto other marketing positions. He is currently the Vice President of Marketing at Custom Direct, where his responsibilities include product development, licensing, sales, and marketing of direct-to-consumer financial products.

Ken Hill

Ken Hill was born and raised in a small town in the Catskill Mountains of New York state. After graduating from high school and being a little car crazy, off he went to California to become a "car designer." He received his degree in Industrial Design as a Transportation major at The Art Center College of Design. Unfortunately, in the early seventies Detroit didn't need any additional designers, so on to the next best thing: Toys. What better than working for a toy company designing "cars"? Hill joined Aurora Products, in West Hempstead, New York, to design Model Motoring/AFX slot cars and accessories, as well as a few kits. In 1983, Matchbox was in need of a designer to work with the United Kingdom and Hong Kong offices to get Matchbox back on track. Through his years at Matchbox, Hill has worked on most of the products in the line, such as the Matchbox 1-75 series, Flash Force, Hot Rod Racers, World's Smallest, Convoy, Skybusters, World Class, Premiere, Feature Vehicles, Large Scale, and Matchbox Collectables, just to name a few.

Berdj Mazmanian

Berdj Mazmanian was born on June 27, 1963, in Beirut, Lebanon. He was exposed to Matchbox from a very early age because his father used Matchbox cars on his Tri-Ang/Hornby HO train layout. In 1969, Berdj's parents decided to relocate the family to the United States as most of their relatives had done before. They chose the Philadelphia area and proceeded to raise their three children in America. Berdj went on to get his degree in Specialized Technology for Electro-Mechanical Design. Having worked in the drafting and design fields, he developed products for everything from electronic connectors to medical equipment. His die-cast experience started with his position as a designer at The Franklin Mint, developing not only vehicle replicas but also making products in pewter, crystal, and other home décor items. In June 1995, he was lured to Matchbox with the promise of starting development of newly tooled products for the fledgling Matchbox Collectibles line. Having started with the direct-marketed line of products, Mazmanian developed tools for such big licenses as Coca-Cola, Harley-Davidson, Jack Daniel's, Jim Beam, Budweiser and Miller

Brewing Co., as well as Mack, Peterbilt/Kenworth, Ford, General Motors, and Chrysler. Today, Mazmanian is Senior Manager of Design responsible for all adult retail products within the Matchbox brand.

The Matchbox Timeline

Listings in roman type are events in Matchbox history.
Listings in *italics* are events in world history.

1947
Lesney Products (inventors of Matchbox) is founded.
The term "cold war" is coined.

1948
Lesney sells die-cast toys to Woolworth's.
The first McDonald's restaurant opens.

1949
Lesney signs marketing agreement with Moko.
The Lone Ranger *debuts on TV.*

1950
Lesney introduces Royal State Coach.
Korean War begins.

1951
Rodney Smith leaves Lesney Products.
I Love Lucy *is an instant success.*

1952
33,000 Large Coronation Coaches sold; 1 million miniature Coronation Coaches sold.
Jack Odell creates first "Matchbox" model.
Eisenhower elected president.

1953
First Matchbox series produced (four models).
Korean War ends.

1954
Emil & Richard Kohnstam register "Matchbox" name.
GM produces its fifty millionth car.

1955
David Yeh joins Louis Marx Company in Hong Kong.
"Rock Around the Clock" is #1 on the charts.

1956
Models of Yesteryear line introduced at Toy Trade Fair.
Elvis Presley records three hit records.

1957
Yesteryear, coined by Jack Odell, is added to dictionary.
U.S. and U.K. commemorate 350th anniversary of first English settlement in America.

1958
Metal wheels replaced with plastic wheels—called "Regular Wheels."
America goes crazy for the Hula Hoop.

1959
Lesney buys Moko and "Matchbox" name.
Barbie is introduced.

1960
Lesney goes public; stock oversubscribed.
JFK wins presidency.

1961
Matchbox introduces glazed windows.
Bay of Pigs invasion ends.

1962
Second series 1929 Bentley features seven die-

cast components.
Cuban Missile Crisis resolved.

1963
Introduction of first Lesney blister packs in United States.
Kennedy confers American citizenship upon Winston Churchill.

1964
Lesney Products U.S.A. formed, with Fred Bronner as president.
Beatles invade America.

1965
First change of color for Models of Yesteryear line.
Cassius Clay beats Sonny Liston for heavyweight championship.

1966
Lesney receives its first Queen's Award to Industry.
Ronald Reagan elected governor of California.

1967
Lesney listed in the Guinness Book of Records.
Green Bay Packers beat Dallas Cowboys in Super Bowl I.

1968
Leslie Smith donates Matchbox models to the Helium Centennial Committee in Texas for time capsules to be opened in 1993, 2018, 2058, and 2968.

Stanley Kubrick lauded for 2001: A Space Odyssey.

1969
SuperFast models launched in response to Hot Wheels.
America places a man on the moon.

1970
Company name changed to Lesney Products Corporation.
Joe Frazier beats Muhammad Ali for heavyweight title.

1971
Lesney begins developing plastic construction kits.
Pentagon Papers published by the New York Times.

1972
Lesney joins Formula Two Motor Racing.
Nixon visits Red China, is re-elected, then besieged by Watergate.

1973
National power strike and fire at factory hit Lesney hard.
U.S. leaves Vietnam.

1974
Lesney enters doll market with "Fighting Furies" and "Disco" girls.
Hank Aaron blasts 715th home run.

1975
Models of Yesteryear line introduced in U.S.
Sony VCRs invade the U.S.

1976
The Shovel Nose Tractor first appears in Matchbox 1-75 range and goes on to become the longest running model in the line.
United States celebrates 200th anniversary.

1977
Lesney acquires Vogue Dolls from Tonka.
Alaska oil pipeline completed.

1978
Lesney acquires A.M.T., U.S. manufacturer of plastic construction kits.
American hot air balloon 1st to cross Atlantic.

1979
Production of Dinky Toys ceases and doesn't resume until Matchbox buys Dinky in 1987.
U.S. and Soviet Union sign Salt II treaty.

1980
Jack Odell comes out of retirement to rejoin Lesney, and Universal begins producing Matchbox models.
Ronald Reagan wins presidency in landslide.

1981
Universal forms "Macau Diecasting Toys Ltd."
IBM introduces its personal computer.

1982
Universal International buys Matchbox Toys out of Lesney receivership.
First artificial heart implant.

1983
Matchbox International formed and first space "Matchbox Toys" model introduced—the Y13-3 Crossley, Carlsberg.
Cable TV subscribers reach 25 million in U.S.

1984
Matchbox 1-75 series expanded to 100 models in Japan.
Bruce Springsteen releases Born in the U.S.A.

1985
Lesney name removed from all Matchbox models.
Pete Rose beats Ty Cobb's record for most hits.

1986
Matchbox Toys declared #1 bestseller in Europe.
American Voyager plane is first to cicumnavigate the globe without refueling.

1987
Universal Matchbox Group buys Dinky.
Johnny Carson Show celebrates 25th anniversary.

1988
Universal Matchbox products now sold in 120 countries.
Cold War ends.

A recent steamroller lines up beside its first counterpart

1989
First Dinky (Matchbox) prototypes shown at U.K. toy fairs.
George Bush inaugurated as U.S. president.

1990
First attempt at mail-order business in U.S. declared a disaster.
McDonald's opens first restaurant in U.S.S.R.

1991
Corgi operations moved to Mattel headquarters in Leicester, England.
Operation Desert Storm a dramatic success.

1992
Matchbox Toys sold to Tyco Toys.
Clinton defeats Bush in presidential election.

1993
Tyco unveils first line of "Matchbox by Tyco."
Bush and Yeltsin sign START 2 treaty.

1994
Alex Welch hires Mike Dukes to run Matchbox Collectibles.
First international worldwide web conference.

1995
Mattel sells Corgi.
Pope John Paul II Time "Man of the Year."

1996
Mattel Toys acquires Tyco Toys and the Matchbox brand.

Princess Diana agrees to divorce.

1997
Matchbox Collectibles reaches peak of $45 million in sales
Tiger Woods wins Masters.

1998
Mattel introduces a new line called "Real Talkin."
VW introduces the new Beetle.

1999
Mattel decides to increase Matchbox 1-75 series to 100 models in major markets.
The Dow reaches 10,000 points for the first time.

2000
Matchbox 1-100 series organized in twenty themed segments of five vehicles each.
150th anniversary of Jack Daniel's birth.

2001
Mattel enters into licensing agreements with interactive companies to develop games and software based on brands including Matchbox.
Hijacked airliners attack World Trade Center and Pentagon.

2002
Mattel issues fifty-model "Matchbox Across America 50th Birthday Series" line.
Queen Elizabeth II celebrates fifty years on the throne.

The Matchbox Club

Matchbox Toys Ltd. asked Kevin McGimpsey and Stewart Orr in 1984 to establish an official but independent collectors club.

These two enthusiastic collectors formed The Matchbox International Collectors Association (M.I.C.A.) as the official collectors club. The club was tasked with publishing a magazine every eight weeks covering the main Matchbox ranges, current, obsolete, and future releases and to be a channel of communication between the manufacturer and the collector. The magazine, all in full color, was originally forty pages but went to forty-eight pages in 1999.

M.I.C.A. is and remains an international organization with branches in North America, the U.K., and Australia. It presently has a membership in excess of 3,000.

M.I.C.A. North America covers USA and Canada:
P.O. BOX 28072
Waterloo, Ontario
Canada N2L 6J8
Telephone: (519) 885-0529

M.I.C.A. U.K. covers UK and Europe:
P.O. BOX 120
Deeside CH5 3HE
Telephone: [01] 244 539414
E-mail: kevin@matchboxclub.com

M.I.C.A. Australia covers Australia, New Zealand, and the South Pacific:
P.O. BOX 26
Winston Hills NSW 2153
Australia
Telephone: (612) 8824 8570

Matchbox models regularly covered in the M.I.C.A. magazine include: Matchbox Miniatures (1-75); Models of Yesteryear and Dinky; Matchbox Collectibles series as well as most of the obsolete ranges made since 1948.

An interesting feature of the M.I.C.A. magazine is the auction of members' rare and unusual Matchbox models. Generally each magazine has more than 150 lots, each one accurately described and individually photographed. This is just one benefit of being a M.I.C.A. member because the auction is only open to members and is a great way to enlarge your collection, sell it, and to gauge the ups and downs of the market. The most expensive model to sell at auction so far was a unique model made by the Matchbox research and development department in the early 1990s to promote the *Budgie* film. It sold for £1,376 ($2,000) in May 2001!

There is also a social aspect to M.I.C.A. Each year M.I.C.A. organizes at least two Matchbox conventions. These are good fun and usually M.I.C.A. takes over a hotel for the weekend. There are plenty of Matchbox toys and models on sale, there are interesting talks on the hobby, and the Saturday culminates in a dinner and auction of rare models.

Kevin McGimpsey and Stewart Orr have both written several books on aspects of the Matchbox hobby:

Collecting Matchbox Diecast Toys –The First 40 Years was first published in 1989 and remains one of the best books ever written on Matchbox.

The Yesteryear Book 1956 to 2000 covers in great detail every model ever made and attributes an accurate price guide to every entry.

Collectors interested in joining the club should contact their nearest M.I.C.A. office or visit us at http://www.matchboxclub.com.

Trademark Listing

AAA is a registered trademark of the American Automobile Association.

A-Class is a registered trademark of Mercedes-Benz Aktiengesellschaft Corp.

Ahrens-Fox Fire Engine is a registered trademark of Ahrens-Fox Fire Engine Company.

Airbus is a registered trademark of Deutsche Airbus Gmbh Ltd.

Air France is a registered trademark of Compagnie Nationale Air France Corporation.

Albertson's is a registered trademark of Albertson's, Inc.

Alvis is a registered trademark of Alvis PLC Public Ltd.

Amoco is a registered trademark of Amoco Oil Co.

American Airlines is a registered service mark and trademark of American Airlines, Inc.

American Girl is a registered trademark of The Pleasant Company.

Anheuser-Busch is a registered trademark of Anheuser-Busch, Inc.

Antiques Roadshow is a service mark of the British Broadcasting Corporation.

Arco is a registered trademark of Atlantic Richfield Co.

Aston Martin is a registered trademark of Aston Martin Lagonda Ltd.

Audi is a registered registered trademark of Audi Ag Corporation.

Austin Powers is a registered trademark of New Line Productions, Inc.

BBC is a registered trademark of the British Broadcasting Corporation.

Beck's has applied for a trademark by Brauerei Beck Gmbh & Co. Kaiserbrauerei Gmbh & Co, Ohg.

Beefeater is a registered trademark of Allied Domecq Spirits & Wine Ltd.

Beetle is a registered trademark of Volkswagen Aktiengesellschaft Corporation.

Bel Air is a registered trademark of General Motors Corporation.

Bentley is a registered trademark of Bentley Motors Ltd.

Big Bird is a registered trademark of Jim Henson Productions, Inc.

BMW is a registered trademark of Bayerische Motoren Werke Aktiengesellschaft Co.

Boeing is a registered trademark of The Boeing Company.

Bronco is a registered trademark of Ford Motor Company.

Budweiser is a registered trademark of Anheuser-Busch, Inc.

Bugatti is a registered trademark of Bugatti International S.A.

Bugs Bunny is a registered trademark of Time Warner Entertainment Company, L.P.

Buick is a registered trademark of General Motors Corporation.

Cabbage Patch Kids is a registered trademark of Original Appalachian Artworks, Inc.

Cadbury is a registered trademark of Cadbury Ltd Corp.

Cadillac is a registered trademark of General Motors, Inc.

Camaro is a registered trademark of General Motors Corporation.

Campbell's Soup is a registered trademark of CSC Brands, Inc.

Carlsberg is a registered trademark of Anheuser-Busch, Inc.

Casio is a registered trademark of Casio Keisanki Kabushiki Kaisha DBA Casio Computer Co., Ltd.

Castlemaine XXXX is a registered trademark of Castlemaine Perkins, Ltd.

Caterpillar is a registered trademark of Caterpillar, Inc.

Cessna is a registered trademark of The Cessna Aircraft Company.

Champion is a registered trademark of Champion Spark Plug Co.

Chef Boyardee is a registered trademark of American Home Food Products, Inc.

Chevelle is a registered trademark of General Motors Corporation.

Chevrolet is a registered trademark of General Motors, Inc.

Chevy is a registered trademark of General Motors, Inc.

Children's Television Workshop is a registered trademark of Children's Television Workshop Corp.

Citröen is a registered trademark of Automobiles Citröen Corp.

Claas is a registered trademark of Claas Ohg Partnership.

Coca-Cola is a registered trademark of The Coca-Cola Company.

Consolidated is a service mark of Consolidated Freightways Corporation.

Cookie Monster is a registered trademark of Jim Henson Company, Inc.

Corvette is a registered trademark of General Motors, Inc.

Cougar is a registered trademark of Ford Motor Company.

Daf is a registered trademark of Daf Trucks N.V.

Daffy Duck is a registered trademark of Time Warner Entertainment Company, L.P.

DaimlerChrysler is a registered trademark of DaimlerChrysler Ag.

Danbury Mint is a registered trademark of Mbi, Inc.

Datsun is a registered trademark of Nissan Jidosha Kabushiki Kaisha Corporation.

"Days Gone" is a registered trademark of Lledo, Ltd.

Dewar's is a registered trademark of Bacardi & Company Ltd.

Dinky is a registered trademark of Kenner Parker Toys, Inc.

Disney is a registered trademark of Disney Enterprises, Inc.

Dodge is a registered trademark of Chrysler Corporation.

Drambuie is a registered trademark of Drambuie Liqueur Co., Ltd.

Du Pont is a registered trademark of E. I. Du Pont De Nemours and Company.

Duckhams is a registered trademark of Alexander Duckham & Co., Ltd.

Dunlop is a registered trademark of DNA (Housemarks) Ltd. Corp.

Esso Petroleum is a registered trademark of the Exxon Mobil Corp.

Evian is a registered trademark of Societe Anonyme des Eaux Minerales d'Evian, S.A.

Fairlane is a registered trademark of Ford Motor Company.

Federal Express and FedEx are registered service marks and trademarks of Federal Express Corporation.

Ferrari is a registered trademark of Ferrari S.P.A.

Firestone is a registered trademark of Bridgestone/Firestone Resarch, Inc.

Ford is a registered trademark of Ford Motor Company.

Ford Expedition is a registered trademark of Ford Motor Company.

Ford F-100 is a registered trademark of Ford Motor Company.

Ford GT is a registered trademark of Ford Motor Company.

Ford Mustang is a registered trademark of Ford Motor Company.

Fordson is a registered trademark of Ford Motor Company.

Formula One is a registered trademark of Formula One Licensing B.V.

Private Ltd. Co.

Franklin Mint is a registered trademark of Franklin Mint Company.

Freddy Krueger is a registered trademark of New Line Productions, Inc.

Freightliner is a registered trademark of Freightliner Corporation.

Frisbee is a registered trademark of Wham-O, Inc. Corporation.

Fuller's is a registered trademark of Fuller Smith & Turner Plc.

General Motors is a registered trademark of General Motors Corporation.

Getty is a registered trademark of Getty Tm Corp.

Ghia is a registered trademark of Ghia S.P.A.

GMC is a registered trademark of General Motors Corporation.

Goodyear is a registered trademark of The Goodyear Tire & Rubber Company.

Goofy is a registered trademark of Disney Enterprises, Inc.

Grand Cherokee is a registered trademark of DaimlerChrysler Corporation.

Grand Prix is a registered trademark of General Motors Corporation.

Greyhound is a registered trademark of Greyhound Lines, Inc.

Grove is a registered trademark of Grove U.S. LLC.

Grumman is a registered trademark of Grumman Corporation.

GTO is a registered trademark of General Motors Corporation.

Guinness is a registered trademark of Arthur Guinness Son & Company Ltd.

Harley-Davidson is a registered trademark of H-D Michigan, Inc.

Harrods is a registered trademark of Harrods Ltd.

Harry Potter is a registered trademark of Time Warner Entertainment Company.

Hasbro is a registered trademark of Hasbro Industries, Inc.

His Master's Voice is a registered trademark of RCA Corporation.

Hispano Suiza is a registered service mark and trademark of Societe Nationale d'Etude et de Construction de Moteurs d'Aviation.

HMV is a registered service mark of EMI Group Canada, Inc.

Holden is a registered trademark of Holden's Motor Overseas Corporation.

Hula-Hoop is a registered trademark of Wham-o Mfg. Co.

Hummer is a registered trademark of General Motors Corporation.

I Dream of Jeannie is a registered trademark of Columbia Pictures Industries, Inc.

I Love Lucy is a registered trademark of CBS Inc.

Ikarus is a registered trademark of Mogurt Kereskedelmi Reszvenytarsasag Company.

Impala is a registered trademark of General Motors Corporation.

Indy is a registered trademark of Indianapolis Motor Speedway Corporation.

Isuzu is a registered trademark of Isuzu Jidosha Kabushiki Kaisha Ta Isuzu Motors Ltd. Corporation.

Jack Daniel's is a registered trademark of Jack Daniel's Properties, Inc.

Jaguar is a registered trademark of Jaguar Cars Ltd.

J&B is a registered trademark of Justerini & Brooks Ltd.

Jeep is a registered trademark of DaimlerChrysler Corporation.

Jim Beam is a registered trademark of Jim Beam Brands, Co.

John Deere is a registered trademark of Deere & Company Corporation.

Johnny Walker Whisky is a registered trademark of John Walker & Sons Ltd Company.

Ken is a registered trademark of Mattel, Inc.

Kellogg's Corn Flakes is a registered trademark of Kellogg Company.

Kenworth is a registered trademark of Paccar Inc DBA Kenworth Truck Company.

K Mart is a registered trademark of Kmart Properties, Inc.

Kodak is a registered trademark of Eastman Kodak Company.

Lagonda is a registered trademark of Aston Martin Lagonda Ltd.

Lamborghini is a registered trademark of Automobili Lamborghini Holding S.P.A.

Land Rover is a registered trademark of Land Rover Company.

Langendorf is a registered trademark of Interstate Brand West Corporation.

Laphroaig is a registered trademark of James Burrough Distillers Ltd. Corporation.

Le Mans is a service mark and trademark of Automobile Club de L'Ouest de la France (A.C.O.).

Libby's is a registered trademark of Societe des Produits Nestle S.A.

Lincoln Zephyr is a registered trademark of Ford Motor Company.

Lincoln is a registered trademark of Ford Motor Company.

Lindt is a registered trademark of Chocoladefabriken Lindt & Sprungli AG.

Lipton Tea is a registered trademark of Lipton Investments, Inc.

Lockheed is a registered trademark of Lockheed Martin Corporation.

"The Lone Ranger" is a registered trademark of Lone Ranger Television, Inc.

Looney Tunes is a registered trademark of Timer Warner Entertainment Company, L.P.

Lowenbrau is a registered trademark of Lowenbrau AG.

Mack and Mack Trucks are registered trademarks of Mack Trucks, Inc.

Magna Doodle is a registered trademark of Pilot Corporation of America.

Martell is a registered trademark of J. & F. Martell, Inc.

Maserati is a registered trademark of Ferrari S.P.A.

Mayflower is a registered service mark of Mayflower Transit, Inc.

Mazda is a registered trademark of Mazda Motor Corporation.

McDonald's is a registered trademark of McDonald's Corporation

McDonald's Happy Meal is a registered trademark of McDonald's Corporation.

Mercedes and Mercedes-Benz are trademarks of Mercedes-Benz Aktiengesellschaft Corporation.

"Mickey Mouse Club" is a registered trademark of Disney Enterprises, Inc.

Michelin is a registered trademark of Michelin North America, Inc.

Miller Brewing is a registered trademark of Miller Brewing Company

Mitsubishi is a registered trademark of Mitsubishi Jukogyo Kabushiki Kaisha Corporation.

M&M is a registered trademark of Mars, Inc.

Morris Minor is a registered trademark of Mobil Oil Corporation.

Mustang is a registered trademark of Ford Motor Company.

Mustang Cobra is a registered trademark of Ford Motor Company.

Nascar is a registered service mark and trademark of National Association For Stock Car Auto Racing, Inc.

Nestlé is a registered trademark of Societe des Produits Nestlé S.A.

"New York Times" is a registered trademark of New York Times Company.

Newcastle Brown is a registered trademark of Scottish & Newcastle PLC Corporation.

Nickelodeon is a registered trademark of Viacom International Inc.

Nintendo is a registered trademark of Nintendo of America Inc.

Nippon Airways is a registered service mark of All Nippon Airways Co., Ltd.

Nissan is a registered trademark of Nissan Jidosha Kabushiki Kaisha Ta Nissan Motor Co., Ltd.

Oscar (The Grouch) is a registered trademark of Jim Henson Productions, Inc.

Oreo is a registered trademark of Nabisco Brands Company.

Ovaltine is a registered trademark of Novartis Nutrition Corporation.

Panzer is a registered trademark of Panzer Motorcycle Works LLC.

Pee Wee Herman is a registered trademark of Herman World, Inc.

Pennzoil is a registered trademark of Pennzoil Products Company.

Pepsi is a registered trademark of Pepsico, Inc.

Perrier is a registered trademark of Perrier Vittel S.A.

Peterbilt is a registered trademark of Paccar Inc.

Pickfords is a registered service mark of Pickfords Ltd. Corporation.

Pininfarina is a registered trademark of Pininfarina International S.A. Corporation.

Piper is a registered trademark of New Piper Aircraft, Inc.

Pirelli is a registered trademark of Pirelli S.P.A. Corporation.

Plymouth is a registered trademark of Chrysler Corporation

Pontiac is a registered trademark of General Motors Corporation.

Pontiac Firebird is a registered trademark of General Motors Corporation.

Popeye is a registered trademark of Hearst Holdings, Inc.

Porsche is a registered trademark of Dr. Ing. H.C.F. Porsche Aktiengesellschaft.

Raleigh is a registered trademark of Derby Holding Ltd. Corporation.

Renault is a registered trademark of Renault Corporation.

Rice Krispies is a registered trademark of Kellogg Company Corporation.

Ringling Brothers and Barnum & Bailey Circus is a registered service mark of Ringling Bros.-Barnum & Bailey Combined Shows, Inc.

Road Runner is a registered trademark of Time Warner Entertainment Company, L.P.

Rolls-Royce is a registered trademark of Rolls-Royce PLC.

Rolls-Royce Silver Ghost is a registered trademark of Rolls-Royce Motors Ltd. Corporation.

Ronald McDonald is a registered trademark of McDonald's Corporation.

Royal Mail is a registered trademark of Post Office, The Parliament, United Kingdom

Rubik's (Cube) is a registered trademark of Seven Towns Ltd.

Saab is a registered trademark of Saab Automobile AB Association.

Scania is a registered trademark of Scania CV Aktiebolag Corporation.

Seagrave is a registered trademark of FWD Corporation.

Sears is a registered trademark of Sears, Roebuck and Co. Corporation.

Scooby Doo is a registered trademark of Hanna-Barbera Productions, Inc.

Scout is a registered trademark of International Truck Intellectual Property Company, LLC.

Scuderia-Ferrari is a registered trademark and service mark of Ferrari Idea S.A.

See's Candy is a registered trademark of Columbia Insurance Company.

Sega is a registered trademark of Sega Corporation.

Sesame Street is a registered trademark of Children's Television Workshop Corporation.

Setra is a registered trademark of Karl Kassbohrer Fahrzeugwerke GMBH Ltd.

Shell is a registered trademark of Shell Oil Company.

Silver Cloud is a registered trademark of Rolls-Royce Motor Cars Ltd. Corporation.

Sinclair is a trademark of the Sinclair Corporation.

Skittles is a registered trademark of Mars, Inc.

Skylark is a registered trademark of General Motors Corporation.

Spitfire is a registered service mark of Spitfire Aviation, Inc.

Steinlager is a registered trademark of Lion Nathan Ltd. Corporation.

Stutz Bearcat is a registered trademark of Stutz Motor Car of America, Inc.

Sunoco is a registered trademark of Sunmarks, Inc.

Suze is a registered trademark of Pernod Ricard.

Target is a registered service mark and trademark of Target Brands, Inc.

Taystee is a registered trademark of American Bakeries Company.

The Texas Company is a registered trademark of Texaco Inc.

Texaco is a registered trademark of Texaco Inc.

Thunderbird Ford is a registered trademark of Ford Motor Company.

Toblerone is a registered trademark of Kraft Jacobs Suchard (Schweiz) Corporation.

Tonka is a registered trademark of Hasbro, Inc.

Toyota is a registered trademark of Toyota Jidosha Kabushiki Kaisha Ta Toyota Motor Corporation.

Trans Am is a registered trademark of Sports Car Club of America, Inc.

Triumph is a registered trademark of Bayerische Motoren Werke Aktiengesellschaft Corporation.

Tyco is a registered trademark of Tyco Industries, Inc.

Unimog is a registered trademark of DaimlerChrysler AG Corporation.

Universal is a trademark of Universal Brands Company, Inc.

U.S. Postal Service is a registered trademark of United States Postal Service.

Vauxhall is a registered trademark of Vauxhall Motors Ltd. Corporation.

Vogue Dolls is a registered trademark of Vogue Doll Company, Inc.

Acknowledgments

The author wishes to thank the following individuals for their invaluable input and advice: Ned Barrett, Rob Butkiewicz, Jim Carty, Vince D'Angelo, Jim Dickinson, Mike Dukes, Chris Guest, Ken Hill, Simon Iredale, Bill Kerner, Everett Marshall, Berdj Mazmanian, Kevin McGimpsey, Nick Mitchell, Jeff Muckler, Stewart Orr, Jim Pisors, Rich Plescia, Ira Rubien, Andrew Tallis and Alex Welch. I also want to thank my editor, Terence Maikels, for providing direction, encouragement, and wordsmithing.

While many of the people who had a significant impact on Matchbox history are mentioned in this book, many who worked behind the scenes in design, engineering, packaging, and other capacities are not mentioned. While a complete list of these people would fill a small phone book, we do wish to acknowledge the contributions of the following: Mike Arenstein, Brian Bailey, Rug Burad, Anita Choy, Ludwig Darmstaedter, Richard Herd, Martin Hickmore, Stanley Kam, Stella Ko, Sunny Lai, Kevin Lam, Vincent Lam, H. S Lee, K. F. Lee, Jimmy Leung, P. O. Liew, Keith Lister, K. C. Lo, Andreas Schaefer, Sid Sullivan, John Torrance, and Derek Wong.

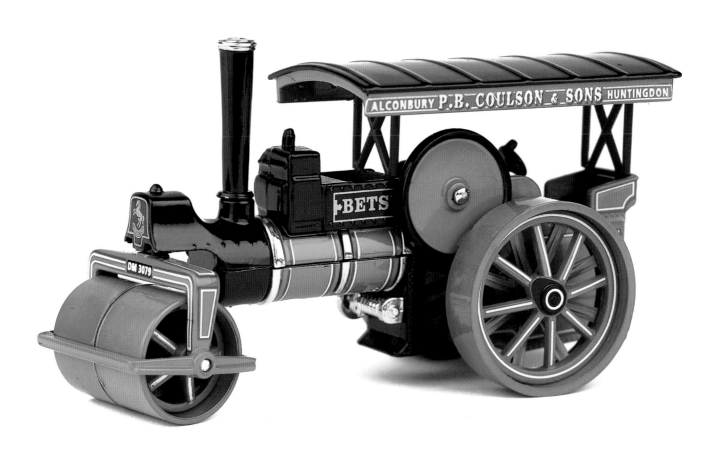

About the Author

Richard J. Scholl has been a consultant, award-winning creative director, and author who has written about collectibles and the industry for more than fifteen years. He has written numerous articles on collecting and was managing editor of *The Matchbox Collector*, a newsletter published by Matchbox Collectibles for many years. Scholl worked full-time for The Franklin Mint for several years and has since developed advertising and reference material for many of America's most prominent direct marketers of collectibles, including The Hamilton Collection, Lenox, Bradford Exchange, Action Performance, Ashton-Drake Galleries, Disney, America Remembers, and Matchbox Collectibles. Scholl has also worked for toy companies including Tyco Preschool and Tyco R/C. A published poet, Richard is the author of *The Running Press Glossary of Baseball Language*, and he has been a research consultant and contributor to many other books. An adjunct professor of communications at Drexel University for eighteen years, he is president of The Scholl Group, a full service advertising, communications, and marketing firm. He earned his Bachelor of Arts degree in Writing and his Masters Degree in English from the Pennsylvania State University. Born in Pittsburgh, Richard now resides in Bryn Mawr, Pennsylvania, with his wife, Catherine, and two children, Geoffrey and Jennifer.